The author has an undergraduate degree in law and criminology, a postgraduate degree in general law and a MSc degree in psychology. The author is a life-long creator turned tutor who enjoys motivating people across the world, teaching and inspiring others about the joys of life and education.

To my mother, Augustine. Thank you for believing in me without any hint of doubt, thank you for being the brightest light in my life.

Samson Yung-Abu

THE CREATIVE TALENTS NOTEBOOK

My Mentor

AUSTIN MACAULEY PUBLISHERS™

LONDON * CAMBRIDGE * NEW YORK * SHARJAH

A CIP catalogue record for this title is available from the British Library.

ISBN 9781398404274 (Paperback)
ISBN 9781398404281 (ePub e-book)

www.austinmacauley.com

First Published 2022
Austin Macauley Publishers Ltd®
1 Canada Square
Canary Wharf
London
E14 5AA

I would like to thank my parents for their endless support. I would also like to acknowledge Kelly Townsend and her family for their endless support, Mathew Leach for his endless support, Anna Wlottkowska, Glyn Croft, Neil Morley, Nehmiah Browne, Sam Alfred, Kirsty Louise Archer, Mashood Moiden, Jerry Nicholes and his other representative for their endless support in keeping me going all these years. Most importantly I would like to acknowledge Austin Macaulay Publishers; my publishers, for their belief in my work, for their dedication, professionalism and services toward the work. For some of the students who have encouraged my work. All my Instagram followers for applauding my inspirational messages.

Let your thoughts leak onto paper and make a puddle of ideas.

When everything is taken away from us, our story is all we have left. How valuable have you made your story? How creative have you been with life, with living, with you and towards others? Are your memories priceless or pointless? These are intimate core questions we eventually find asking ourselves sooner or later, and in some cases, when it's already too late to make a difference.

Writing is A Single Act of Originality

Ideas are short-lived in our mind but immortal on a blank page.

Creativity Is Bravery: Only the Audacious Mind Braves Change, Only the Courageous Mind Creates Change

It is not the size of the hunter that matters but the mind in the hunter. The rat does not hide in a small hole because it feels that its body is too small but because it feels scared and safe in it. The lion, however, is not the biggest animal in the jungle, but it does not hide in a bigger hole for safety; it does not dwell on its size, but displays itself in the open any time any day, whenever it wants or needs to.

The lion, unlike the rat, does not feel the need to hide in a hole for safety, just because it feels smaller than other animals. In his own mind, it feels its own strength and ability to meet any challenge head on: to eat when it wants, to think when it wants, to do when it wants, to walk when it wants, to make an appearance when it wants and to be free in its own natural surroundings. It feels safe in his own mind, rather than unsafe in his surroundings.

That is what makes the lion the king of the jungle, not because of its size but its mindset. Both animals are hunters but only one lives scared and hidden. Which hunter are you? We are all creators but only few are brave enough to get started, to get great, to get known.

Author's Note

Your reality could be hell. But when you have a burning imagination in your mind, you have a pleasant place, a heaven, to revisit every day.

But firstly, one must ask this very critical question: why this notebook? To understand the purpose of a notebook or a book, one has to know what it solves or provides. What does it solve? What does it provide? This is a plausible question because, as humans: to use anything efficiently, one has to understand why we have to have it and how it can benefit our living standards.

So what does it provide? In short, it provides two things. First, it provides an environment conducive for dreamers. In its broadest sense, this notebook gives thoughts, emotions, ideas, imagination and hunches a secure, safe and inspirational place to flourish. This notebook, metaphorically speaking, is a soil for growing thoughts, ideas and imaginations. Metaphorically speaking, it is like an incubator that enables your ideas to mature to its full extent.

Secondly, it provides motivation through life-changing inspirational quotes designed to motivate you while you work on your dreams. This is because motivational quotes are a source of rich experience and knowledge captured in a few words to explain what successful people have done in the past to produce winning inventions around the world. These motivational quotes take you out of your mind to think. For creators, for dreamers, for inventors, musicians, authors and the like, there is no better way to stay motivated than having a notebook in your possession and at your disposal that is mobile and readily available.

At the end of the day, we are all dreamers; they are our originality, our true identity. Dreams are imaginations capable of taking any individual to a destination called invention if nurtured right in a conducive environment with the right mentality.

Right now, imagine being where you've always wanted to be in your mind. That picture of success that you've ever imagined in your world. You see, imagination is the fairy-tale of the mind. It is the story, the reality, we want to share with the world. In the purest form, imagination is the maker of innovation. It is triggered by a desire to influence change. Imagination is the burning desire to break, make and redefine history.

However, to convert imagination to invention, one must become like a scientist. One must create a better environment (a lab) for it to grow, one must visit it daily on a platform such as a notebook or a journal (under a microscope), reflect on it, ponder it, tweak it. One must apply courage, belief, a tremendous amount of consistent and constant willpower and hard work.

Due to this definition, I had this imagination, this craving to create a routine where people are readily inspired to generate more ideas within a short space of time. To work on their craft with efficiency, improve them and produce only original work in the process. It is now with great pleasure that I have stumbled on this particular idea to create this inspirational notebook.

I believe that winning innovation is inevitable when imagination takes shape on a blank page and revisit daily with an inspired mind that craves a change capable of filling a need in the world dedicated to constant changes. So this made it easier for me to answer the next question.

What does this notebook solve? It solves the fear and the lack: the fear of never daring your imagination, of never taking it further across to the finish line. Most imagination that happens in our mind never makes it past the mind. These ideas never mature into any winning innovation; they remain redundant or become extinct to somewhere unknown or to someone else.

So this notebook, in its resourceful, creative, inspiring and adaptive form, is designed to solve the lack of ideas, the lack of dreams, the lack of ambitions, the lack of courage, the lack of talent, the lack of self-control, the lack of healthy mindset, the lack of motivation, the lack of inspiration and the lack of originality.

As humans, our mind is often littered with all sort of life events: problems, challenges, confusion, rejection, inequality, injustice, social pressure, criticism mixed with joy, adventure, achievement, financial plans, ideas, imagination, vision, objectives, emotions, etc., making it not conducive to think with clarity or dream big. This notebook is a conducive creative environment: it provides a beautiful place, a hopeful place to revisit any time, any day.

You can bring your imagination into reality just by writing down your thoughts or sketching out your ideas. These are the building blocks of wining innovation. It is undoubtedly the case that the human brain is the creator of many incredible creations, and we all have a brain, capable of individual original unimaginable imaginations, we just need to summon the courage to use our brain habitually and practically on blank pages.

I must confess that before today, every day, I wasted a million-dollar idea until I started investing them on paper with a pen.

For me, writing is about taking the chains off and unleashing what is yet to be discovered, what the world craves, anew. And we can only unleash what's on our mind better when they are transferred from thought to paper, from ideas to winning innovation.

I wrote down everything that crossed my mind—good, bad and ugly ideas— I wrote them all down in my personalised inspirational journal with one of my inspirational quotes: "Don't wait for a miracle, start an idea." I researched, I analysed, I reflected on my ideas, I refined them and I made something out of them.

I believed in my thoughts, even when many people around me didn't. But because it meant everything to me, I held my head up high and kept my mind working and my hands writing and my imagination flowing. I wanted so badly to get my message across, no matter what. I am telling you, you can break the norm and take off if only you dare to see yourself in the sky above the skyscrapers.

It was no coincidence that I received a publishing contract for my last book *Student Exam Passport* within a short period. It was all down to penning thoughts and ideas on paper over the years, believing in them and believing that someone out there with the right resources and the right courage will appreciate my work. Try it and see for yourself! Get writing, and now!

Writing, as we should know, is at the centre of human connection; it is a gift of universal unity and critical understanding. We must all observe that words are essential to everyday living, everyday improvement, and the art of writing sits at the centre of human connection. The ability to think, write and create from the mind is a gift to be nurtured day in day out. It is collective enjoyment. We should seek ways to encourage ourselves and others to harness this skill, wherever we might be, wherever they might be.

Creativity is Reserved for the Audacious Mind

Self-Creation, Mental Health, Writing and Journaling: A Letter to All Creative Thinkers or Beginners

There is always another part of the full story, the good part: it is easier to remember the negative part of our past life if we don't spend time reflecting on the whole part of our past living.

Dear creative thinkers,

I would like to thank you all for picking up *The Creative Talents Notebook*. Warning, be creatively cautious, this book might just become your most valuable possession of all time. A positive mind is highly essential during any creative process, which is why this letter is essential, this is what makes *The Creative Talents Notebook* that extra unique.

You see, a positive mind will always find a way to pull you through tough creative times. When you are inspired, you discover a different you, a stronger you. You develop a different kind of happiness: you become driven and fuelled with motivation that the thought of quitting gets forgotten during critical stages in the creative process.

As an author, I learnt first-hand that happiness is what we find when we spend time discovering ourselves, when we engage in expressive writing, when we delegate the burden of thinking to writing on to a blank page. The truth is, a blank page is a good listener. A blank page helps us discover all the great things that we haven't thought of in a while, all the great things we haven't been able think of about ourselves.

Many people find it hard to reach any level of happiness in life during their creative journey, and they eventually quit all together due to the burden of stress, depression, anxiety or burnout. There are few critical reasons why many people stop being creative or stop producing or presenting their ideas. One of the reasons is down to the burden of the mind: mental health issues, a negative mindset or negative self-image: *I'm not good enough, people will judge me, my work will never be good enough, I can't get out of bed, I don't have the motivation, my idea is not what people will accept, I don't have the time, I'm afraid I might get it wrong, people will judge me and laugh at me.*

This mentality holds the best and gifted people from expressing exceptional art or other forms of creativity (everyone is precondition to be a creator). However, if we approach creativity energetically, motivated and with a positive mindset of who we are really born to be, like a child would, nothing can stop us from producing what we really care about for the benefit of us or others. Children see creativity as a necessity, a form of true emotion and happiness. Children don't see flaws in their work, for them, whatever they produce is meant to be that way.

Children have the perspective of perfection. And with each work, they grow, they feel, they become. Any creative activity is perfect in its physical form. So, just create. Just start with what you can, ignore the fear of doing it wrong, of being laughed at, of being dismissed and in no time you will start doing what you really want to do.

As a creative thinker myself, I have learnt to appreciate the power of a motivated mind. It is easier to feel content in a small cage when we've spent our entire life feeling safe inside of it, even if the doors have always been off. This is the power of the mind: restrictive or limitless.

While creativity is largely based on passion, handwork and a longing for true purpose in serving ourselves and the world, building a positive person through a positive mind is at the centre of it all. Talent alone without a healthy mindset cannot accomplish anything great. This is one of the primary reasons why most talented and creative minds never go on and work on their crafts.

The first few rules of creativity is having a strong belief, creating true inner happiness and having a positive self-image within ourselves. These are very important assets to take on in our creative journey. We as creator should be a constant part and parcel of our own creative process, whatever that might be.

Our mind should be a place of peace and constant positivity so we don't fall into the little cage of fear, discouragement or self-devaluing. To achieve this, we must also take time out for ourselves: It is paramount to take time out to think about what has been going on in your life till date.

Your best work is never your work, but yourself, and through your best self, you will produce your best work. You really can't give your best if you are not feeling at your best; this is why self-evaluation is highly critical: to give your best, you have to understand yourself. Truth is, we can become our own worst enemy of progress if we don't spend the time to know ourselves, to reflect. Conclusively, we can't expect others to understand us if we don't spend the time understanding ourselves.

The creative person as a golden rule always creates time to reflect on themselves. Many of us have developed the mindset of a hung wall clock: effective, but not to itself. Like the clock, we work 24/7 at the sole benefit of others' living enhancement. We primarily function just to please and serve others because we don't want to be considered selfish or useless. We don't want to be discarded or replaced. We devalue our own potential and opportunity to develop our own ability because we are worried we might be judged or we will never amount to anything better.

We feel guilty for taking time out for ourselves. We often feel like if we don't give others our time, they won't want us anymore. That is the mindset of a hung clock. To be respectfully appreciated, we must put ourselves first; it is not selfish, but self-value. We must create time to work on ourselves, to improve ourselves. key advice to remember is that you can't become first or be valued at anything if you put yourself last every time at everything. True happiness is the conscious act of putting yourself first and others next. Not last, but next.

Apart from its creative platform, *The Creative Talents Notebook* is also a great personal reflective tool as well as an incredible stress management tool. It fosters internal happiness and boosts self-esteem. Through its inspirational nature, users/readers will begin to feel a different sense of belief, confidence and courage and discover their inner true identity, their under-utilised strength, when they commit to using this Notebook for expressive writing (feelings).

Managing overwhelming emotions and reducing anxiety and stress is a common question many people find hard to speak about in our modern society. We feel ashamed to even admit it, to confess what's on our mind to another soul. With writing, we can offload what we are so eager to speak but unable to vocalise, without guilt, without shame or worry.

According to recent psychological research studies, writing is highly therapeutic. Writing facilities creative self-expression and facilitates self-awareness. Writing brings about many healing elements when one engages in the act of writing expressively: writing reduces depression and anxiety; it provides clarity of the mind and cathartic release. Furthermore, if one engages in writing for the purpose of journaling, the same effects are produced. Journaling through expressive writing (writing about how you feel) can help individuals develop a different perspective about themselves and about the world around them. Helping them create a new self-image of themselves.

The Creative Talents Notebook—in its extensive practical form—is also designed as a journaling tool to self-discovery and recovery. Mental health in our modern era is more common than ever, affecting all age around the globe. What *The Creative Talents Notebook* does is it encourages journaling and ensures such self-discovery is done in a positive way and with an inspired mindset.

According to further research, journaling helps the brain regulate emotions as well as keeping your brain in a better working condition. Journaling also improves your overall mood while at the same time instilling in you a greater sense of happiness and general emotional well-being. Journaling helps us analyse the past in the present so we can make better judgments in the future. Once journaling becomes more of a frequent habit, it becomes highly likely that we become better at managing personal adversities or helping others manage theirs through our own reflection or story.

The Creative Talents Notebook is designed in a way that you don't have to feel obliged to write in a certain way or draw in a certain way. It is designed in a way that gives you freedom to write as you please. You don't have to know where to start, you can just write whatever, whenever, wherever. Write about facts, failures, funny things, events and details—anything that comes to mind at any point, at any time.

The Creative Talents Notebook is also personal, so go all out if you must, when you can, don't censor yourself: don't worry yourself with perfection, with punctuation, grammars or spelling anything right, just WRITE! Write about your previous successes and go back and read through them if/when you're feeling low. Remind yourself of past achievements and previous milestones.

I hope in whatever form you choose, you can influence change with *The Creative Talents Notebook*. With this, I conclude my letter.

Best of luck.

Get Up, Grab it and Write it Down, Now!

With writing, you discover what you never thought of before during thinking.

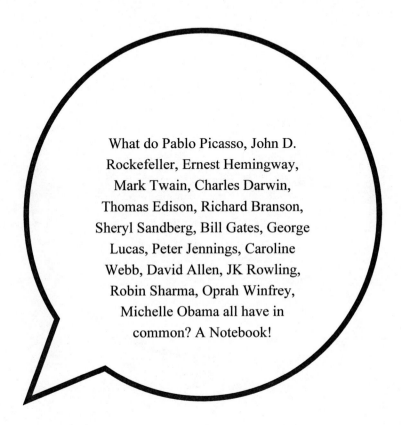

What do Pablo Picasso, John D. Rockefeller, Ernest Hemingway, Mark Twain, Charles Darwin, Thomas Edison, Richard Branson, Sheryl Sandberg, Bill Gates, George Lucas, Peter Jennings, Caroline Webb, David Allen, JK Rowling, Robin Sharma, Oprah Winfrey, Michelle Obama all have in common? A Notebook!

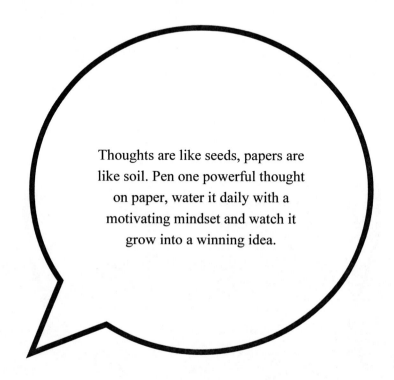

Thoughts are like seeds, papers are like soil. Pen one powerful thought on paper, water it daily with a motivating mindset and watch it grow into a winning idea.

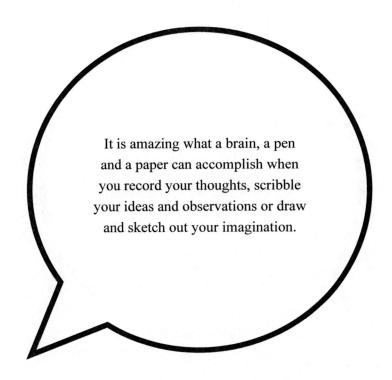

It is amazing what a brain, a pen and a paper can accomplish when you record your thoughts, scribble your ideas and observations or draw and sketch out your imagination.

We don't write down ideas only
so that we don't forget them; we
write down ideas so that they
don't forsake us.

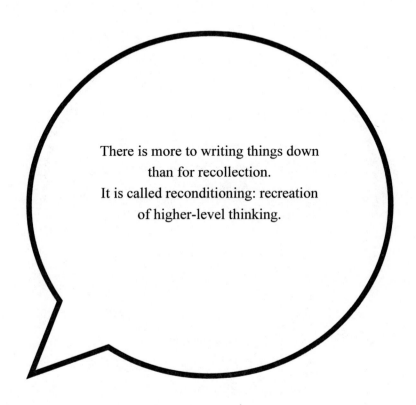

There is more to writing things down
than for recollection.
It is called reconditioning: recreation
of higher-level thinking.

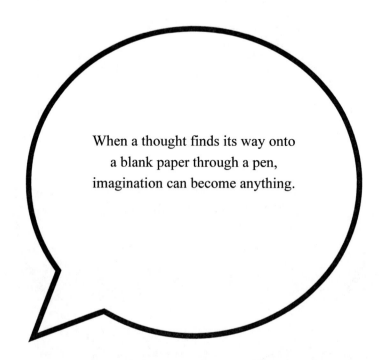

When a thought finds its way onto
a blank paper through a pen,
imagination can become anything.

Write like you know what you are doing; sketch like you've done it a thousand times before; this is how magical things happen.

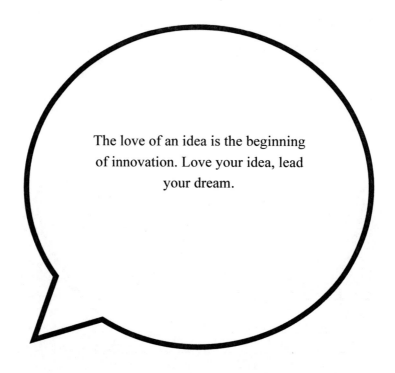

The love of an idea is the beginning of innovation. Love your idea, lead your dream.

Dare to Dream Big or Bigger;
No Permission Necessary!

Thoughts become dangerously valuable on paper; write nothing less than everything.

Creativity is closing your mouth,
opening your mind and going crazy.

Creativity is the foundation of belonging; it is the first sign of identity.

Sometimes, purpose comes after random productivity; keep writing it all down.

Keep reading, keep writing and keep thinking. One day, your actions will get you to triumph.

Your first thought can become your
best invention. Just write it down.
Thoughts, like treasure, are expensive
to waste. Store them in a notebook.

Every day, write something down. At some point, the art of writing will become a routine, then a necessity, then an obsession and then an addiction—then it will become a lifelong craving.

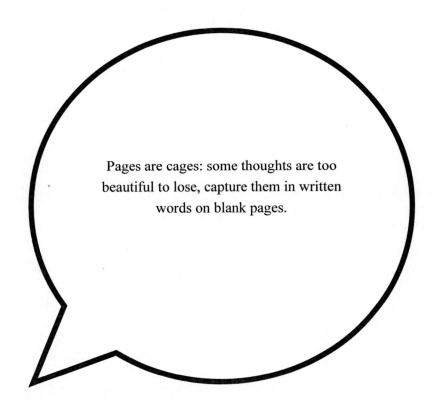

Pages are cages: some thoughts are too beautiful to lose, capture them in written words on blank pages.

Dare it! Envisage it! Visualise it! Realise it! Create it!

Brave your thoughts: innovation does not start until it is on paper.

A blank page is freedom waiting to happen; write your story, edit your reality.

Paper is a fertile soil for planting thoughts and harvesting ideas.

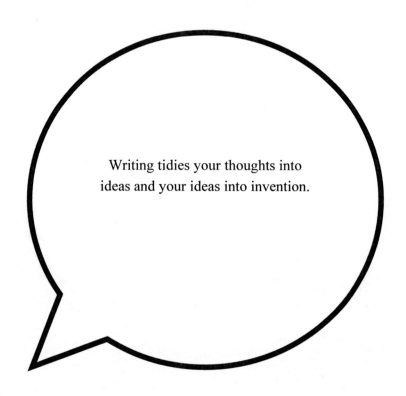

Writing tidies your thoughts into ideas and your ideas into invention.

With a pen and a blank page, your thinking might wander off but your thoughts never get lost.

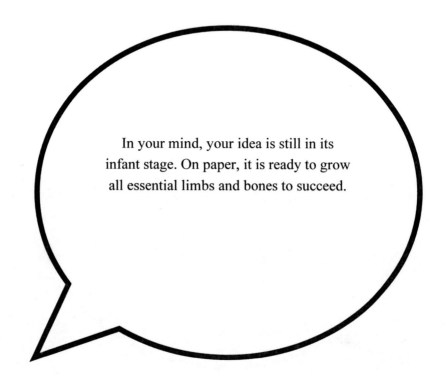

In your mind, your idea is still in its infant stage. On paper, it is ready to grow all essential limbs and bones to succeed.

Brave Your Best!

You don't have to be big; you just have to be bold. You don't have to be strong; you just have to be sure. You don't have to be powerful; you just have to be positive that you've got what it takes to defeat your challenges.

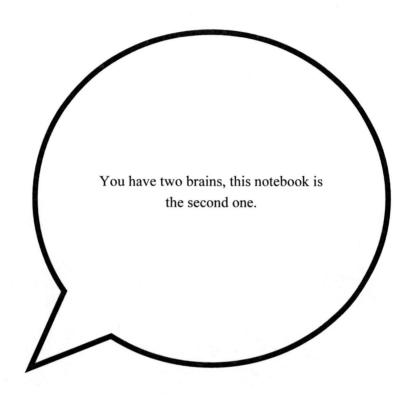

You have two brains, this notebook is
the second one.

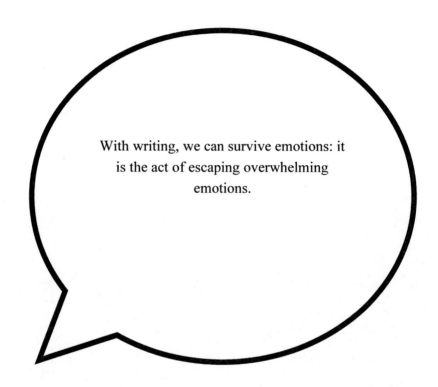

With writing, we can survive emotions: it is the act of escaping overwhelming emotions.

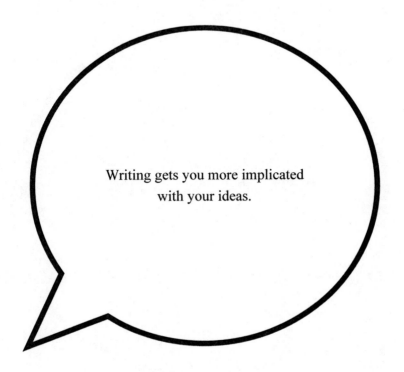

Writing gets you more implicated
with your ideas.

Writing is the safest place to daydream, think and feel.

The only place that thoughts can wander off without getting lost is on blank pages.

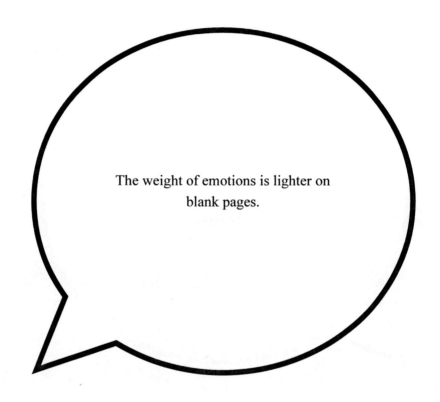

The weight of emotions is lighter on blank pages.

Set Your Mind to a Motivational Mindset!

Motivation does to the mind what food does to the body. It sustains us and provides us with the energy to keep going, to carry on.

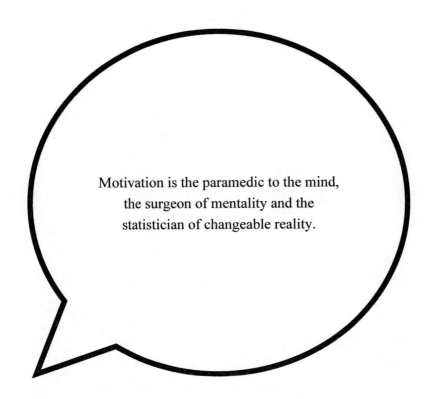

Motivation is the paramedic to the mind, the surgeon of mentality and the statistician of changeable reality.

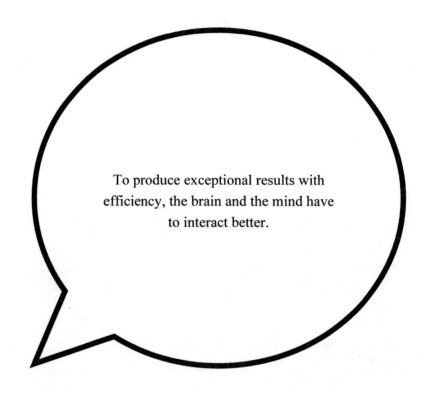

To produce exceptional results with efficiency, the brain and the mind have to interact better.

Only a mind that believes, achieves.
Stay in your motivational zone.

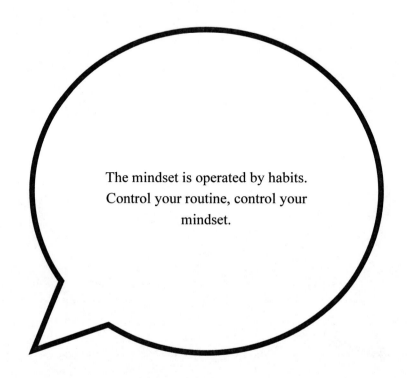

The mindset is operated by habits. Control your routine, control your mindset.

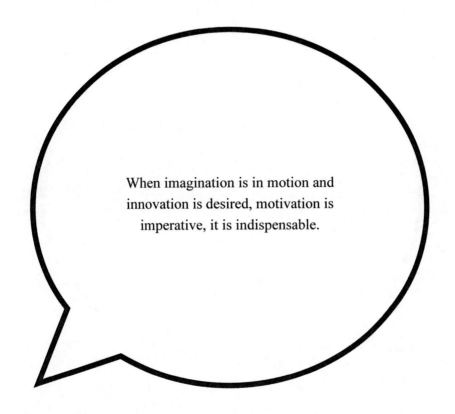

When imagination is in motion and innovation is desired, motivation is imperative, it is indispensable.

Identity is what we become after
developing a mindset.

Mindset is the evidence of habit, good or bad.

Mental Makeover!

Even at the most stressful moments in life, a motivated mindset retains the belief to win.

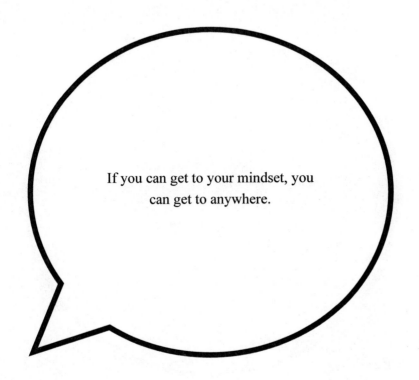

If you can get to your mindset, you
can get to anywhere.

Make motivation a daily necessity, it makes you mentally self-sufficient.

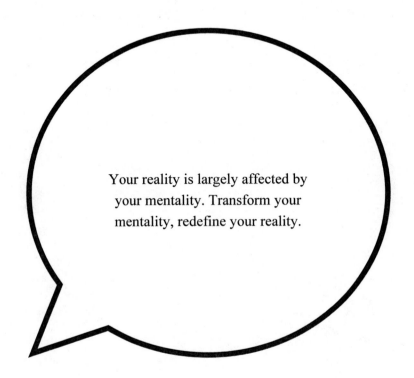

Your reality is largely affected by your mentality. Transform your mentality, redefine your reality.

Motivation is the medicine to a negative mind.

To change, we have to start from the
basic—the mindset.

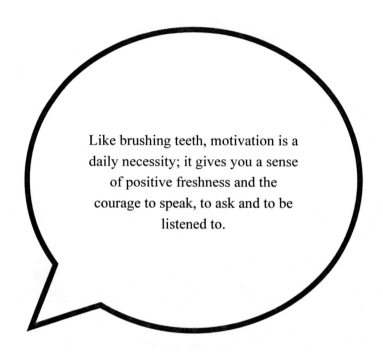

Like brushing teeth, motivation is a daily necessity; it gives you a sense of positive freshness and the courage to speak, to ask and to be listened to.

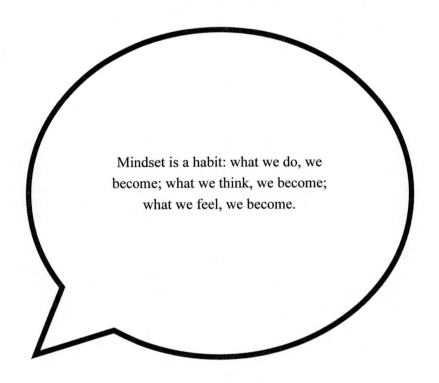

Mindset is a habit: what we do, we become; what we think, we become; what we feel, we become.

Fear Not, Keep Going

Definitely. Not. Afraid.

Failure can be a calling in disguise.
Do it again until they answer.

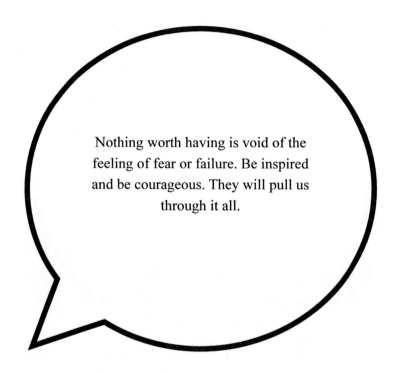

Nothing worth having is void of the feeling of fear or failure. Be inspired and be courageous. They will pull us through it all.

Sometimes it is not the fear inside of us that holds us back. It is the opinion of the people around us that keeps us behind.

Failure is not permanent, regret is.
Keep going.

Failure is an accessory to success.

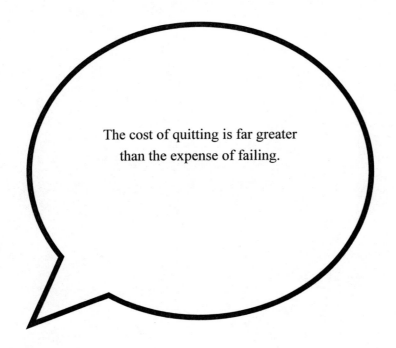

The cost of quitting is far greater
than the expense of failing.

Fear is Overrated!

Be bold to dare fear.

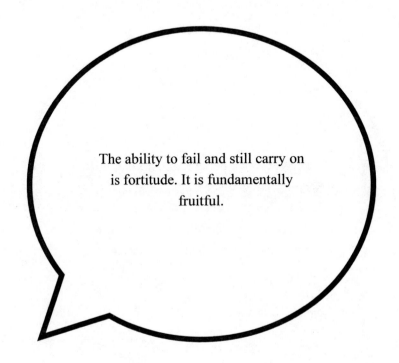

The ability to fail and still carry on
is fortitude. It is fundamentally
fruitful.

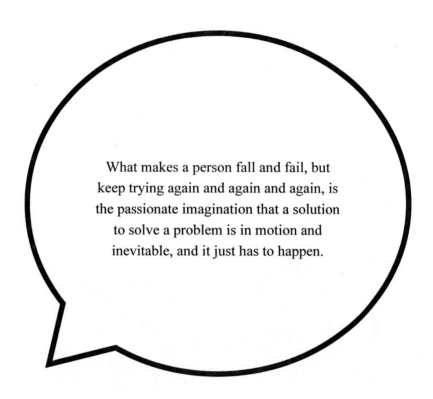

What makes a person fall and fail, but keep trying again and again and again, is the passionate imagination that a solution to solve a problem is in motion and inevitable, and it just has to happen.

Fear is just a costume pulled over success; be courageous, take it off and take off.

Somewhere and anywhere can be day one, so start from anywhere, it is somewhere, make it today, now and start.

Success is little failures added up together over time, mixed with belief and concluded with courage.

Failure is the beginning of success,
it is day one.

Humans are littered with fear, fear is overrated, overused. Recycle fear into fearlessness.

Be Fearless

Failure lures you towards success, not away from it. Keep going, better, stronger.

Failure is not a flaw in creation; it is a foundation, a stepping stone to success.

The bridge from failure to success is the audacity to keep trying.

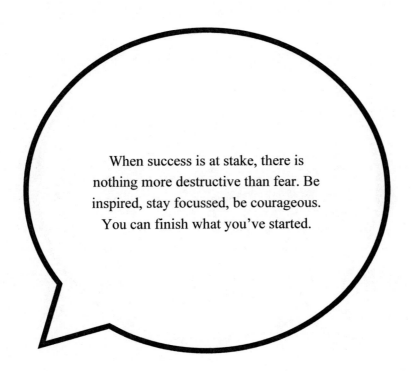

When success is at stake, there is nothing more destructive than fear. Be inspired, stay focussed, be courageous. You can finish what you've started.

Just dare it. Everyone is entitled to happiness.

Failure is an indication of development, not defeat.

Every fall is a foundation to flourish.

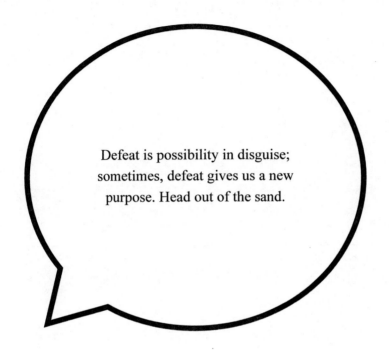

Defeat is possibility in disguise; sometimes, defeat gives us a new purpose. Head out of the sand.

A Reading Mind is a Thinking Mind!

Read, refine your thoughts and redefine your ideas.

Wisdom is the kingdom of wealth.

If you want to go places, sit and read books.

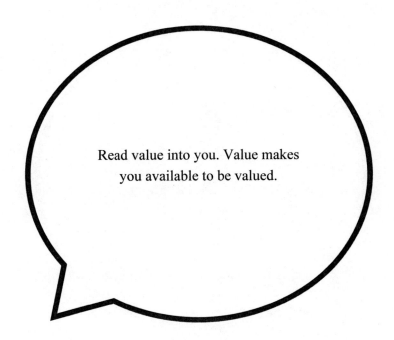

Read value into you. Value makes
you available to be valued.

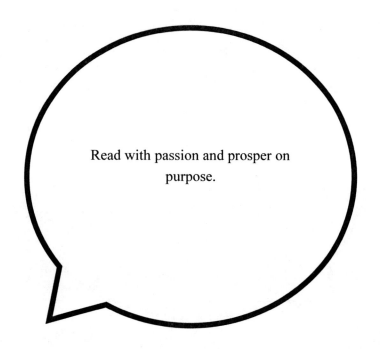

Read with passion and prosper on purpose.

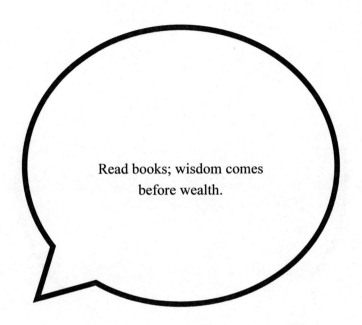

Read books; wisdom comes
before wealth.

Reading gives you the courage to keep going.

Reading improves reactive thinking.

Be Courageous, Be Audacious, Lead Your Thoughts

Belief is the first sign of courage and courage is the first sign of freedom.

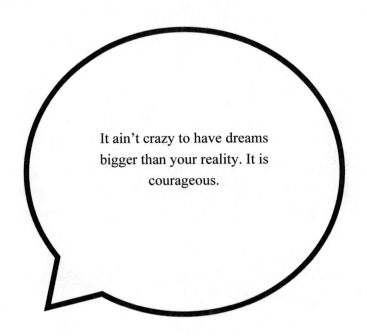

It ain't crazy to have dreams bigger than your reality. It is courageous.

One thing that successful people
have in common is the courage to
dare to dream.

A single act of courage can change
your entire reality.

Courage silences fear; it makes fear ineffective.

Courage transfers fear into fearlessness.

Risk is not just what we do; it is what we don't do. Do what you have to do. Have the courage.

Courage and belief makes
everything worthwhile.

Be Courageous

Courage is the burning desire of hope.

It takes courage to start and belief
to finish.

We are all extraordinary on the inside; some of us just know how to wear our courage inside out.

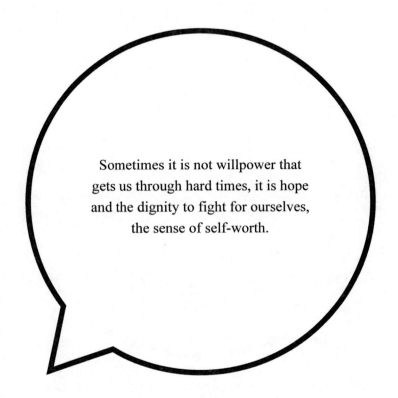

Sometimes it is not willpower that
gets us through hard times, it is hope
and the dignity to fight for ourselves,
the sense of self-worth.

Courage is the bridge between
failure and fortune.

The most courageous act of all is the
act to love and to believe.

Courage is giving yourself the
go-ahead to go ahead.

Always aim high; one accomplishment can change your entire courage.

Read, Lead Your Thinking and Nurture Your Ideas

Reading is the gym of mentality; it enhances your ability and changes your reality.

The love of reading is the beginning
of wealth.

Read books; they are magical, they brave us to change the imposter reality of impossibility.

Read vigorously, read wildly, read with passion. Wisdom is the secret ingredient to a great life of wealth.

Sometimes it takes a book to hatch
you out of your comfort zone into
the life you are destined for.

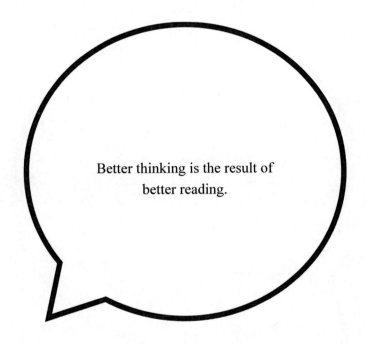

Better thinking is the result of better reading.

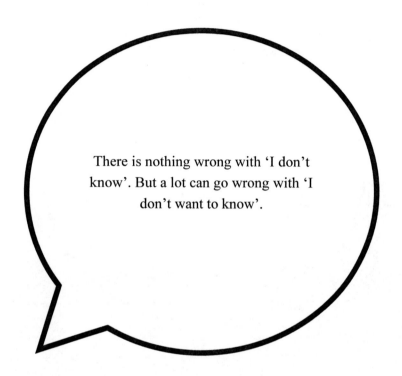

There is nothing wrong with 'I don't know'. But a lot can go wrong with 'I don't want to know'.

Knowledge adds flavour to your mindset.

Believers Become what They Believe

Bet your belief on you. Sometimes, all it takes is believing in what you are becoming.

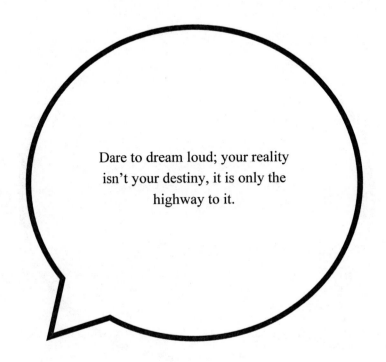

Dare to dream loud; your reality isn't your destiny, it is only the highway to it.

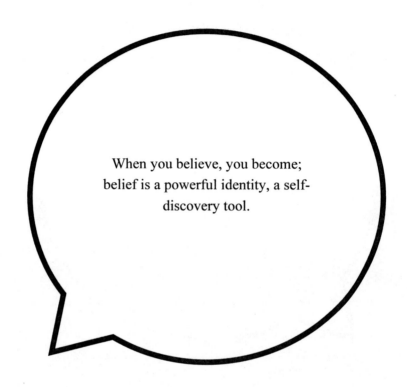

When you believe, you become; belief is a powerful identity, a self-discovery tool.

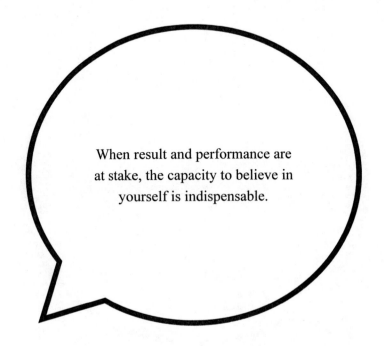

When result and performance are at stake, the capacity to believe in yourself is indispensable.

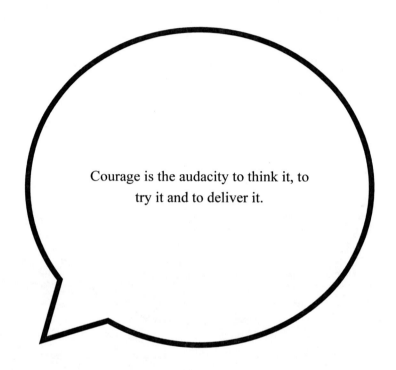

Courage is the audacity to think it, to
try it and to deliver it.

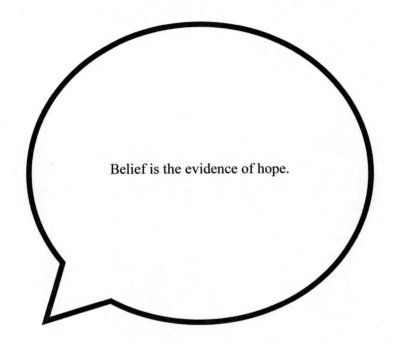

Belief is the evidence of hope.

Belief is the seed of progress.

Keep believing in you; keep working hard on your craft. One day, the right people will believe in you just like you've always believed in yourself.

Listen to Your Calling

Sometimes, you have to listen with your heart, not your ears.

Be careful of the opportunities you let go; you might just have given away your best big idea.

Don't neglect your calling; neglect
is the maker of regret.

There is really something magical
about self-belief.

At first, books take us to beautiful places; then later, they make us a beautiful place to stay in.

Read books; in books, we find the
missing pieces to our lives.

I've always believed that money can't buy time until I started reading books.

With absolute authority, believe you
are no exception to success.

Inscribe Imagination

Innovation is the destination of imagination.

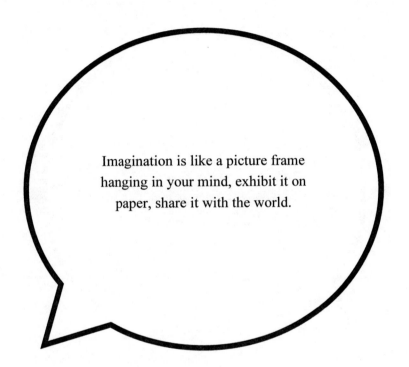

Imagination is like a picture frame
hanging in your mind, exhibit it on
paper, share it with the world.

Imagination is a picture of a different reality, captured on paper in words.

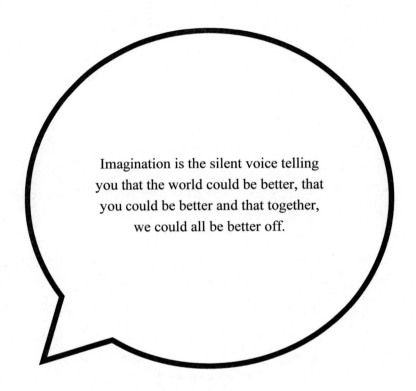

Imagination is the silent voice telling
you that the world could be better, that
you could be better and that together,
we could all be better off.

A person with an imagination is a master in his own right, be merciless with your thoughts, they are your slaves on paper.

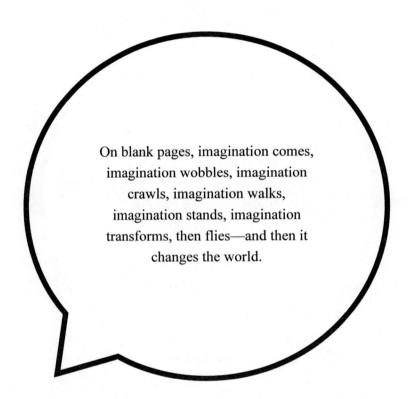

On blank pages, imagination comes, imagination wobbles, imagination crawls, imagination walks, imagination stands, imagination transforms, then flies—and then it changes the world.

The best view of the world is
through your imagination.

Through writing things down, imagination can take the shape of a new reality.

Inscribe Inspiration

You can get started anytime, but to get anywhere worthwhile, you need to be inspired to get there.

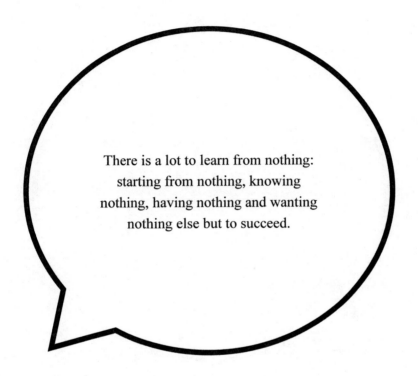

There is a lot to learn from nothing:
starting from nothing, knowing
nothing, having nothing and wanting
nothing else but to succeed.

It is inevitable. When you are
inspired, you innovate.

Create time to think on paper:
improvement is a product of reflection.

Inspiration is all around us, we just have to look around us.

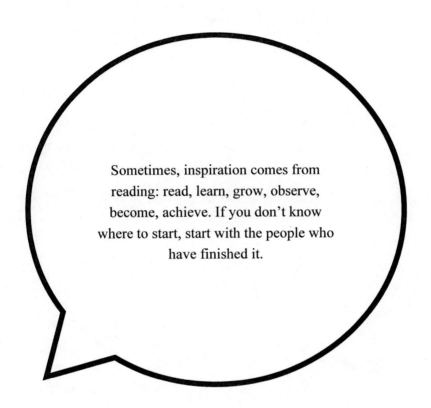

Sometimes, inspiration comes from reading: read, learn, grow, observe, become, achieve. If you don't know where to start, start with the people who have finished it.

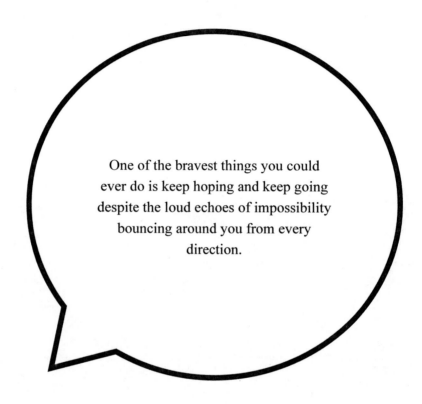

One of the bravest things you could
ever do is keep hoping and keep going
despite the loud echoes of impossibility
bouncing around you from every
direction.

Success is part ability, part belief, part courage, part knowledge, part inspiration.

Learn to Lead

When you are humble to learning, life leads you to infinite wisdom and wealth.

A person that reads, leads. Learn today, lead tomorrow.

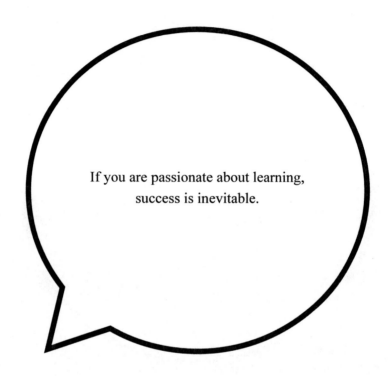

If you are passionate about learning, success is inevitable.

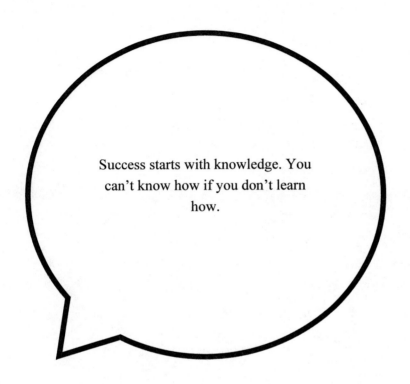

Success starts with knowledge. You can't know how if you don't learn how.

Level up, learn with commitment, lead with excellence.

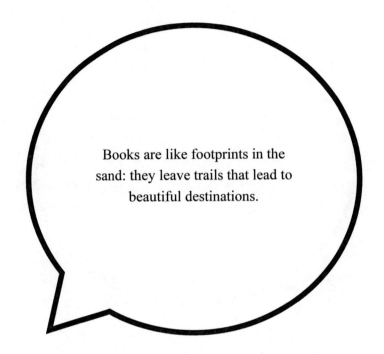

Books are like footprints in the sand: they leave trails that lead to beautiful destinations.

Reading is the act of having a conversation with your mindset.

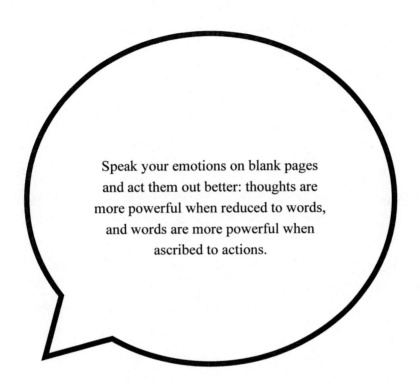

Speak your emotions on blank pages
and act them out better: thoughts are
more powerful when reduced to words,
and words are more powerful when
ascribed to actions.

Inscribe Routine; Inscribe Discipline

A habit breeds more of the same thing. The more you write, the more you write; the more you imagine, the more you imagine; the more you create, the more you create; the more you inspire, the more you inspire. Your actions are always replicating themselves.

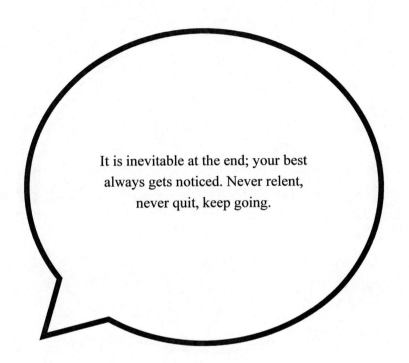

It is inevitable at the end; your best always gets noticed. Never relent, never quit, keep going.

Keep thinking, keep writing and keep reading; one day, your actions will get you to triumph.

Excellence is the result of habits.

Preparation is the key to high performance.

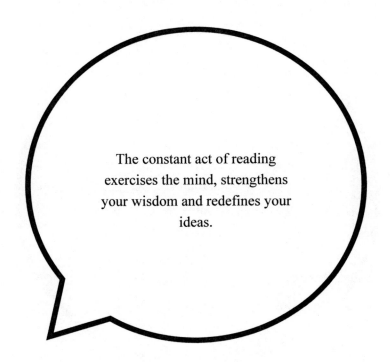

The constant act of reading
exercises the mind, strengthens
your wisdom and redefines your
ideas.

The reward of repetition is excellence.
Repeat the good routine: think again,
read again, imagine again, believe
again and win again.

Practice makes competence and
good habits sustain it.

Inscribe Your Success

The average cost of success is knowledge. Seek wisdom and wealth will result.

Success makes us creators,
keep winning.

Work is what you do, smart is what you become and success is what you acquire in the process.

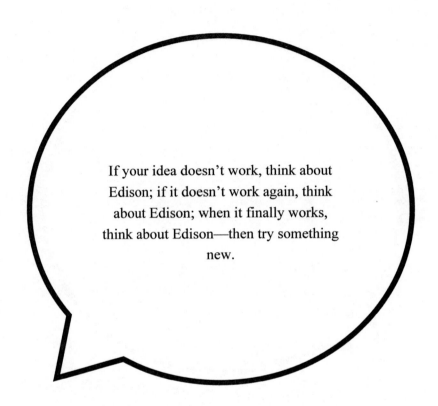

If your idea doesn't work, think about Edison; if it doesn't work again, think about Edison; when it finally works, think about Edison—then try something new.

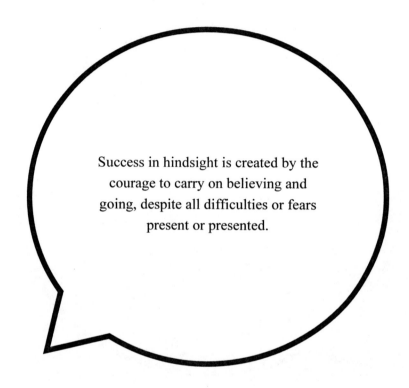

Success in hindsight is created by the courage to carry on believing and going, despite all difficulties or fears present or presented.

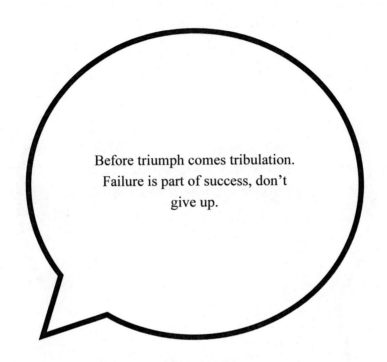

Before triumph comes tribulation.
Failure is part of success, don't
give up.

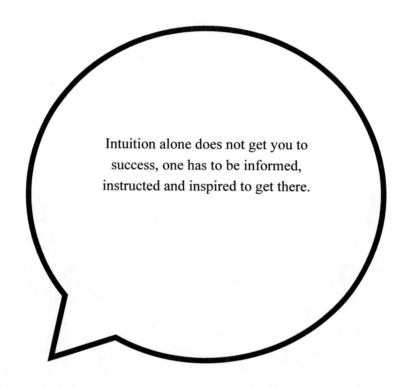

Intuition alone does not get you to success, one has to be informed, instructed and inspired to get there.

Success has no season, just habitual systems.

Narrate Your Story, Create Your Success

Success isn't an accident, it is a calculated risk and it is intentional.

Effort is what takes you from the side-lines to success.

Successful people set three critical
things daily: they set goals, boundaries
and routine.

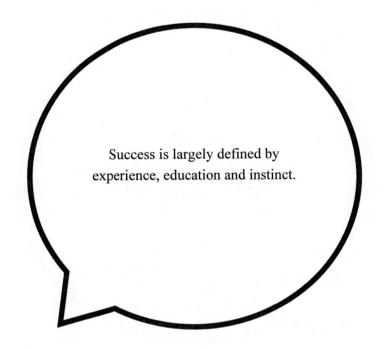

Success is largely defined by
experience, education and instinct.

When you don't stop, you succeed, you win.

Success is a dare. First you dare yourself
to dream it, and then you dare yourself
to deliver it.

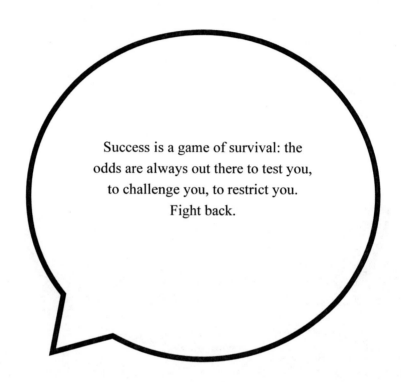

Success is a game of survival: the odds are always out there to test you, to challenge you, to restrict you. Fight back.

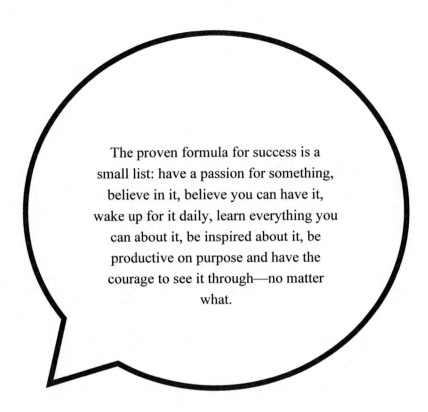

The proven formula for success is a small list: have a passion for something, believe in it, believe you can have it, wake up for it daily, learn everything you can about it, be inspired about it, be productive on purpose and have the courage to see it through—no matter what.

Be Productive. Purposely!

When inspiration is a daily routine, productivity increases and creativity becomes an inevitable consequence: it flows spontaneously.

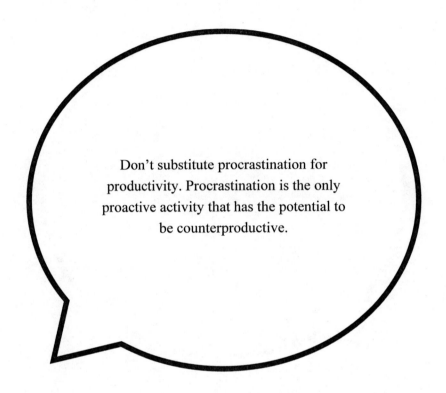

Don't substitute procrastination for productivity. Procrastination is the only proactive activity that has the potential to be counterproductive.

Always be productive on purpose.
When you kill time doing nothing, you
bury opportunity.

You've got to be so active, so creative, so productive that the naysayers and competitors can't keep up.

Tip all your loose thoughts on blank pages, they add up and make a great change.

Writing thoughts down and reading
persistently is the wisest financial
decision you will ever make.

Creativity occurs during intentional productivity.

Your first thought on paper can
become your best invention.

You First

Be always available to you.

It takes courage to become the best
version of you.

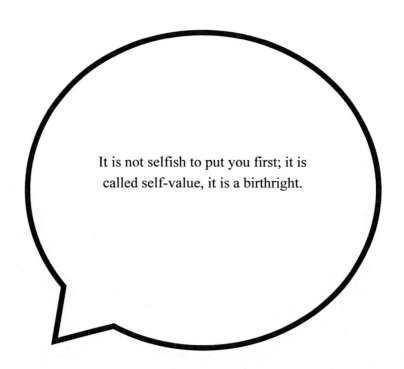

It is not selfish to put you first; it is called self-value, it is a birthright.

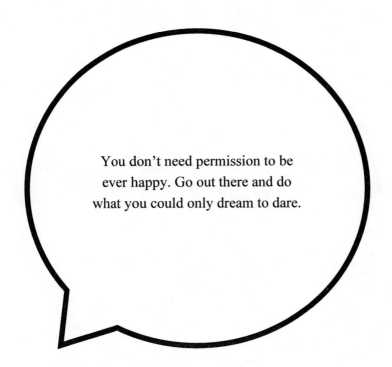

You don't need permission to be
ever happy. Go out there and do
what you could only dream to dare.

Be kind. Daily. Always. A daily act of kindness has the ability to transform you into a happier version of yourself.

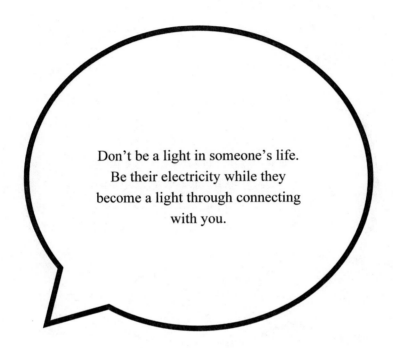

Don't be a light in someone's life.
Be their electricity while they
become a light through connecting
with you.

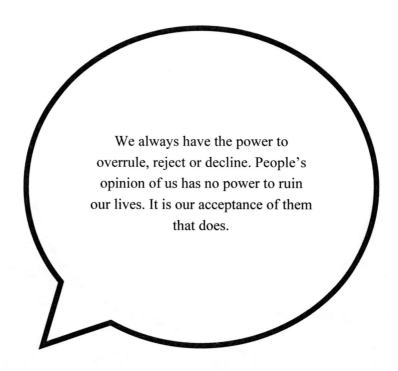

We always have the power to overrule, reject or decline. People's opinion of us has no power to ruin our lives. It is our acceptance of them that does.

Your best days are inside of you.

Trust You, Be Your Inspiration, Inspire You, Through You

Deep down, there is this version of you, in you, who believes in you. Just listen to your inner voice and do it.

Invention is not just about new technology and fancy gadgets; invention can also mean creating a new, better, smarter version of yourself: a more loving, caring, passionate, adventurous, faithful and happy version of you.

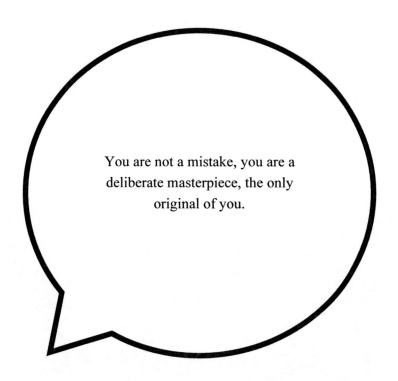

You are not a mistake, you are a deliberate masterpiece, the only original of you.

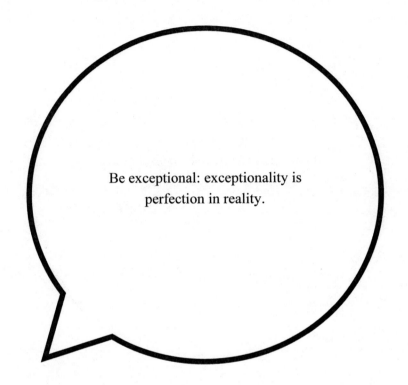

Be exceptional: exceptionality is perfection in reality.

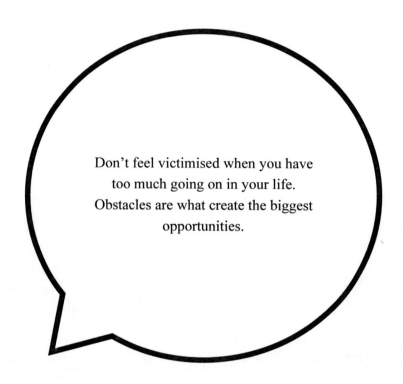

Don't feel victimised when you have too much going on in your life. Obstacles are what create the biggest opportunities.

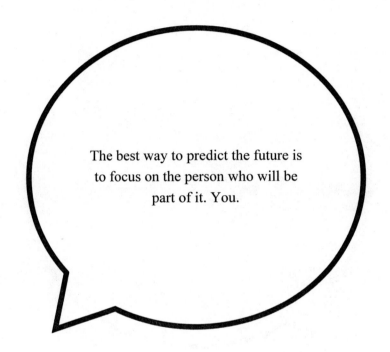

The best way to predict the future is to focus on the person who will be part of it. You.

If you want to have a serious, honest and worthwhile conversation with yourself, write.

Your happiness is your territory; don't let anyone trespass without invitation.

Be an Inspiration to Someone Else

Sometimes, helping others changes us for the better. Change creates change, it is reciprocal.

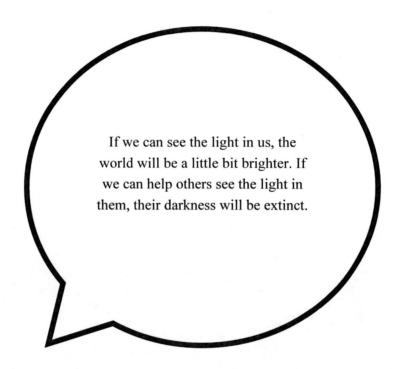

If we can see the light in us, the world will be a little bit brighter. If we can help others see the light in them, their darkness will be extinct.

Give your best, daily, even if you
feel like nobody deserves it.

Kindness is contagious; share it around like a Tweet.

Be the role model your children need.

Stay motivated daily; you might be the
only positivity encounter for someone
else on a single day.

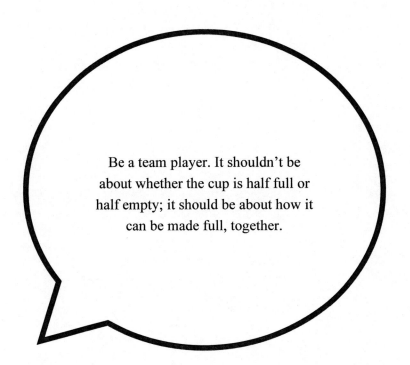

Be a team player. It shouldn't be about whether the cup is half full or half empty; it should be about how it can be made full, together.

Inscribe Love and Happiness

Sometimes, it is not bravery that makes us fight our battles and win; it is love, hope and a longing for happiness.

Family is, above all, wealth. It is the best drive to success, the invention of happiness.

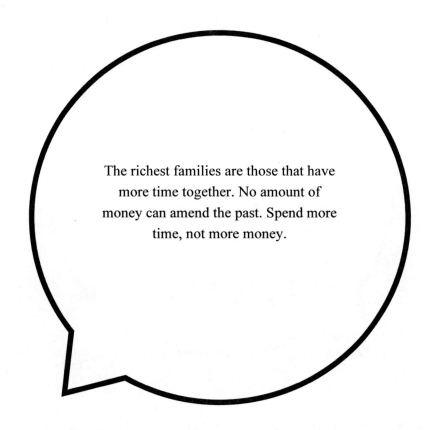

The richest families are those that have more time together. No amount of money can amend the past. Spend more time, not more money.

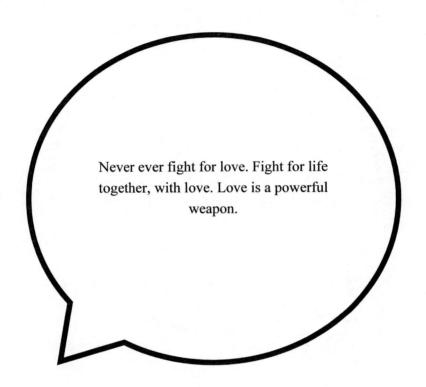

Never ever fight for love. Fight for life together, with love. Love is a powerful weapon.

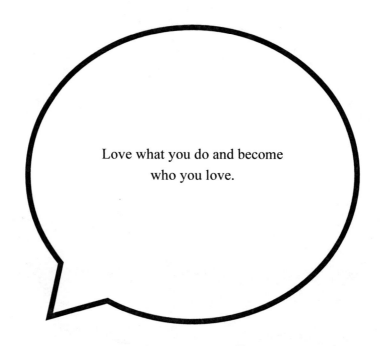

Love what you do and become
who you love.

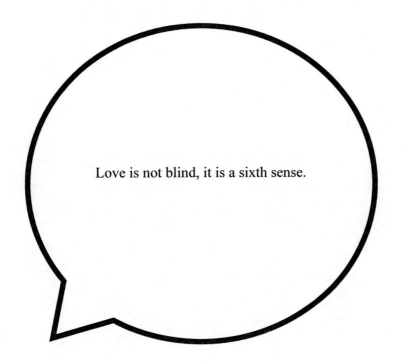

Love is not blind, it is a sixth sense.

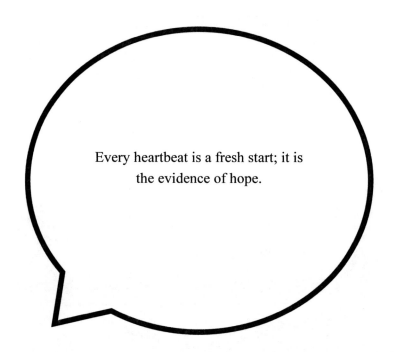

Every heartbeat is a fresh start; it is
the evidence of hope.

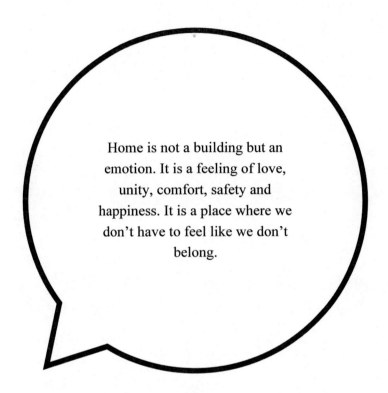

Home is not a building but an emotion. It is a feeling of love, unity, comfort, safety and happiness. It is a place where we don't have to feel like we don't belong.

Inscribe Knowledge

Reading is magical, it instils in us the ability of foresight and a sense of courage that success is possible, that it can be done, that it has been done before and we likewise can do it again.

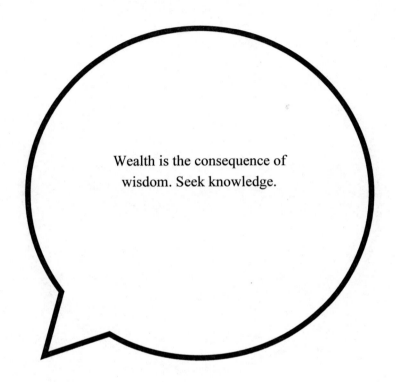

Wealth is the consequence of wisdom. Seek knowledge.

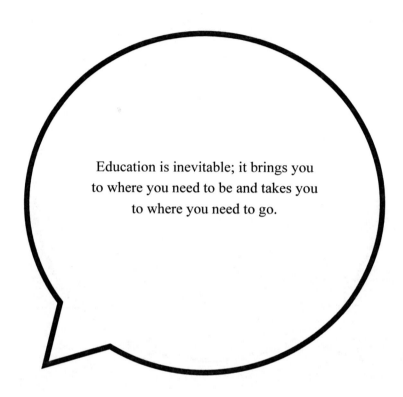

Education is inevitable; it brings you to where you need to be and takes you to where you need to go.

Knowledge eradicates ignorance; it invites acceptance.

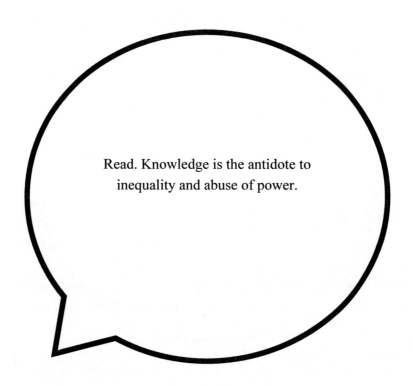

Read. Knowledge is the antidote to inequality and abuse of power.

There is really no greater privilege
in life than the opportunity to be
knowledgeable.

Knowledge is the best immunity
from our inner battles.

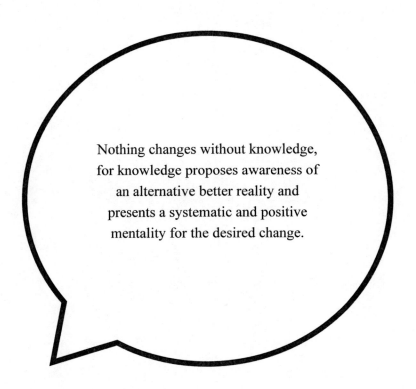

Nothing changes without knowledge, for knowledge proposes awareness of an alternative better reality and presents a systematic and positive mentality for the desired change.

Wake Up, Get Up and Go! Wake Up, Get Up and Go! Wake Up, Get Up and Go!

Do it again.

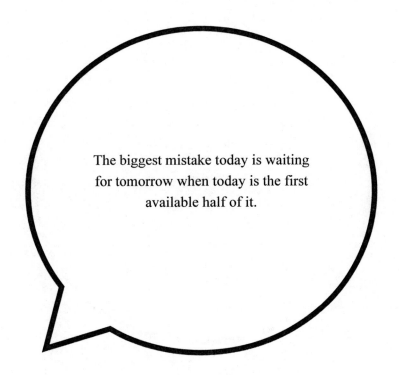

The biggest mistake today is waiting for tomorrow when today is the first available half of it.

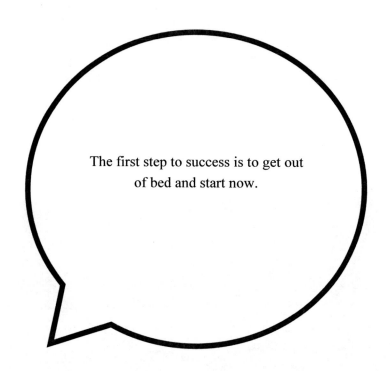

The first step to success is to get out of bed and start now.

Where you are right now is where
you need to be, not where you should
stay. Keep going.

Keep working hard, the right people
will raise you.

Risks bring discomfort but leave comforting rewards behind. Keep going.

Wake up, get up, stand tall, take a deep breath, tell yourself it is going to be a good day today, envisage it, then navigate your narrative accordingly.

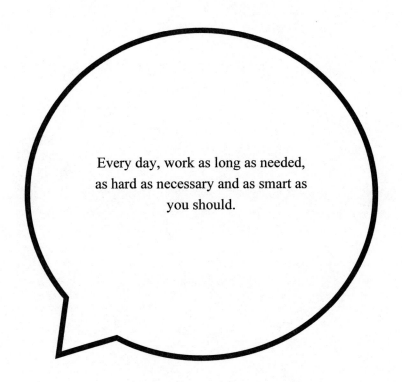

Every day, work as long as needed, as hard as necessary and as smart as you should.

Repeat! Again!

The place we currently are is the result of the limit we've either made or broken.

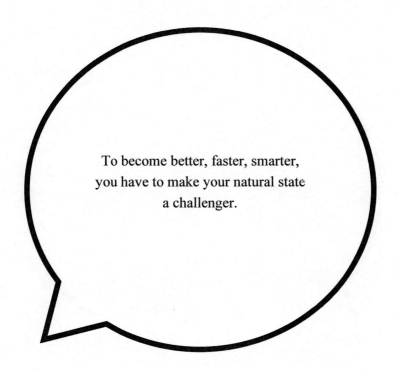

To become better, faster, smarter,
you have to make your natural state
a challenger.

Having a goal makes you wake up each day with a renewed interest in living.

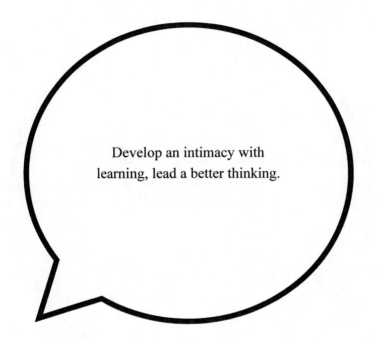

Develop an intimacy with
learning, lead a better thinking.

If you are not willing to explore and expand your experience, you will struggle to excel.

Keep going. The day will come when you will go from minus and negative to plus and surplus.

Today is the rest of yesterday, don't stop, carry on going forward.

Your circumstance might be complicated but it is not conclusive so long as you keep moving forward and remain committed to your goal.

Mind Over Mental Health

Motivation is the mind's survival kit.

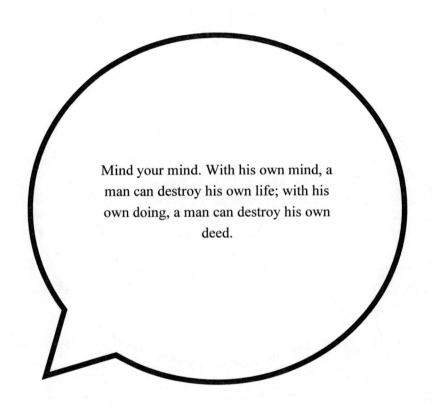

Mind your mind. With his own mind, a man can destroy his own life; with his own doing, a man can destroy his own deed.

A peaceful mind is a free mind.

A blank page encourages a mind to empty itself.

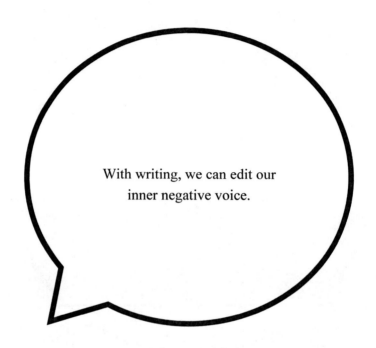

With writing, we can edit our
inner negative voice.

If you can't get out of your bed, get
out of your mind.

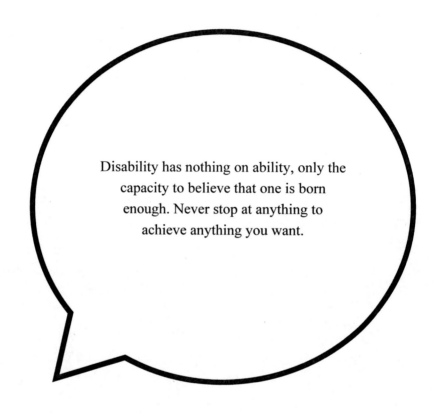

Disability has nothing on ability, only the capacity to believe that one is born enough. Never stop at anything to achieve anything you want.

Only a mind that understands itself
can be understood.

Page Your Mind

Please always give everything.

An inspired mind is the creator's workshop.

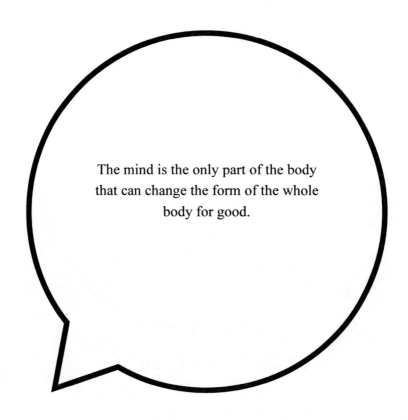

The mind is the only part of the body
that can change the form of the whole
body for good.

A positive mind is a productive mind.

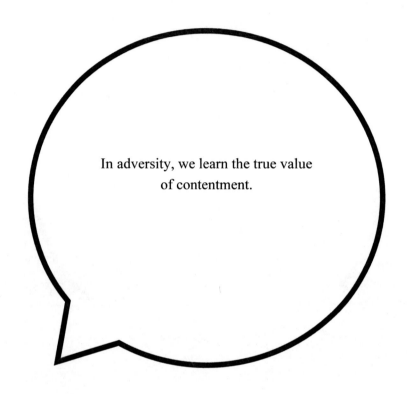

In adversity, we learn the true value of contentment.

Make your own happiness a career, don't just work on your day job, work on your own joy.

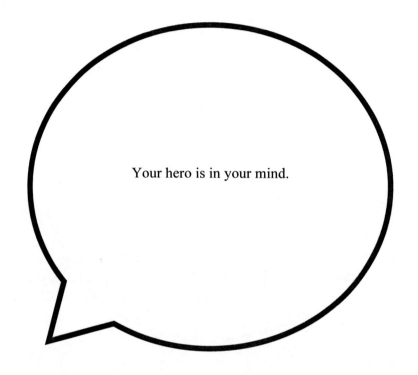

Thoughts are hard to control in our mind, but on paper, they are changeable.

Positive Vibe

The most expensive jewellery to any occasion is a positive mindset: wear your best vibe, always.

In appreciating the little things, we invite more and dine with abundance.

Let your favourite place be your mind, so you can keep all your favourite places in your favourite place.

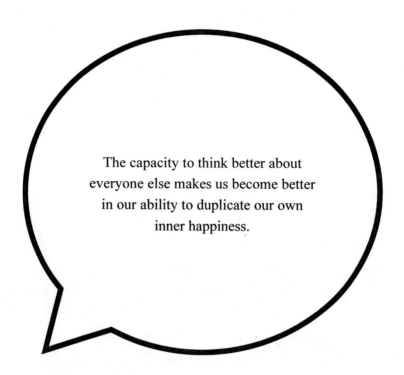

The capacity to think better about everyone else makes us become better in our ability to duplicate our own inner happiness.

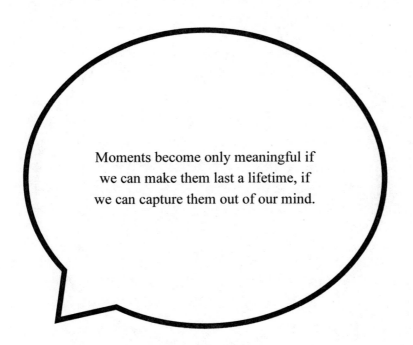

Moments become only meaningful if
we can make them last a lifetime, if
we can capture them out of our mind.

Sometimes, little is enough to express much.

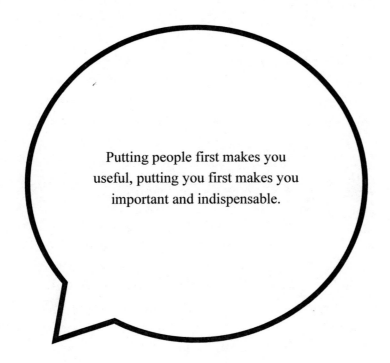

Putting people first makes you useful, putting you first makes you important and indispensable.

Inner Strength!

Don't give up, gear up.

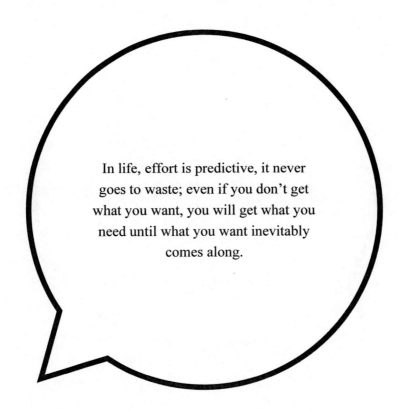

In life, effort is predictive, it never goes to waste; even if you don't get what you want, you will get what you need until what you want inevitably comes along.

In hard work, good news makes an appearance.

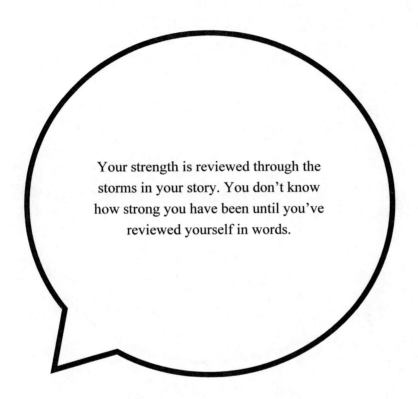

Your strength is reviewed through the storms in your story. You don't know how strong you have been until you've reviewed yourself in words.

Sometimes, we have to make tough decisions after we've made thoughtless ones.

You can't water someone else's
plant and expect yours to grow.

To understand your vision better,
you have to understand your version
better.

The past is your best gift to your future self.

Fulfil You

If you want to be happy, work on something you've always wished you were really great at.

Starting can be scary but it is the
only way to finish.

There is an entrepreneur in everyone, but only a brave mind gets to meet theirs.

Habits are heard to depart from,
make good ones a gift to your
future self.

Burn your fear with the flames of
your burning passion.

Stop living below your problems, and start living up and above your potential.

The side-effect of laziness is regret.

Goodness is the maker of greatness.

Hard Work!

Hard work without inspiration is slavery to the soul.

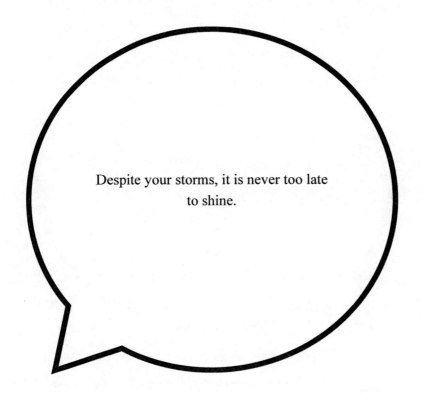

Despite your storms, it is never too late
to shine.

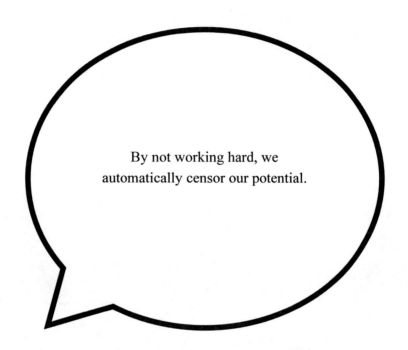

By not working hard, we automatically censor our potential.

The moment we stop creating, we age.

Hard work makes you a bait to opportunities, keep working while you float.

Consume more of what you wish
to become.

Use your obstacles to build a step to
reach your success.
Inspiration instigates improvement.

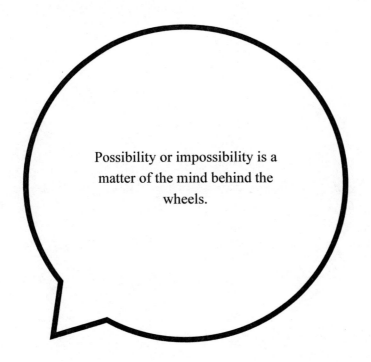

Possibility or impossibility is a matter of the mind behind the wheels.

Hard Work!

Hard work and inspiration combined are the two most important distractions from quitting.

Have the courage of a seed and the
patience of a farmer.

Luck doesn't just come your way,
you invite it through hard work, you
meet it through hard work.

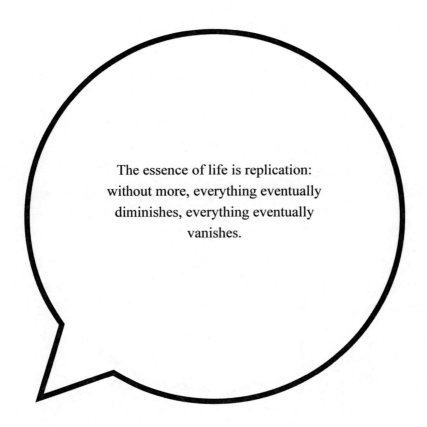

The essence of life is replication: without more, everything eventually diminishes, everything eventually vanishes.

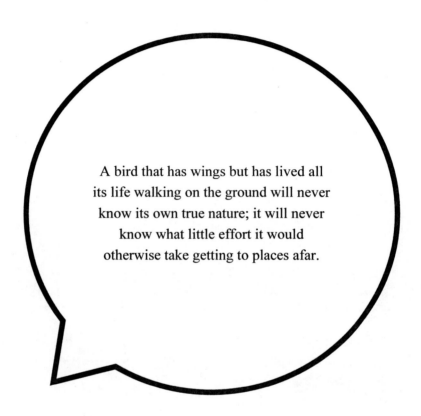

A bird that has wings but has lived all its life walking on the ground will never know its own true nature; it will never know what little effort it would otherwise take getting to places afar.

Some things in life you can't learn
until you've suffered the
consequences.

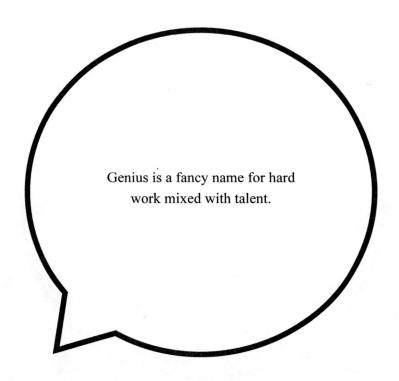

Genius is a fancy name for hard
work mixed with talent.

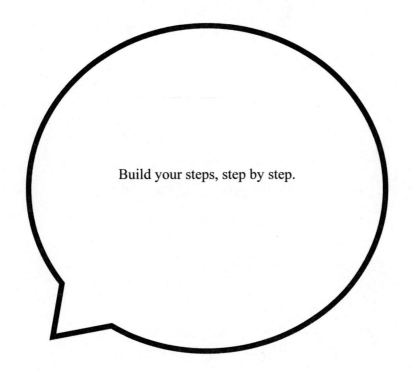

Build your steps, step by step.

Story!

If you can't reflect, you can't recover; you discover your strength through your storms, through your story.

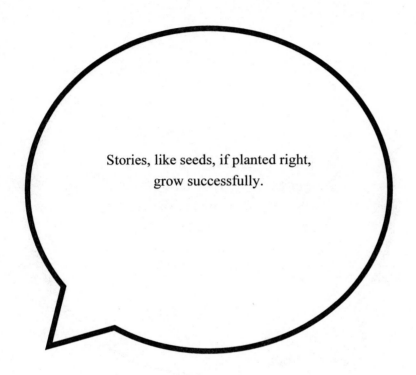

Stories, like seeds, if planted right,
grow successfully.

There are no rules when it comes to creating your own story, just resources; start now, work through your storms, find your voice and discover your success.

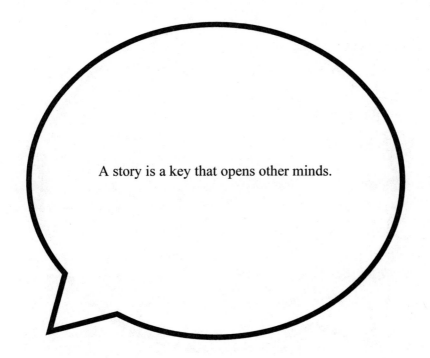

A story is a key that opens other minds.

Success always starts in a storm.

Your past is the solution to your struggle.

Success is a story once created in
storms and transformed into sunshine.

Creativity is not about creating
perfection but about creating
exceptional work with a flawed
mind.

Life!

Let inspiration flourish everywhere.

Two rules of life: capture moments, create memories.

In life, our ultimate success is the storms we get to survive.

In life, the bill of ignorance can cost
you a mountain of collateral damage.

Everything in life is optional,
including living well.

If you are scared of meeting failure,
you will never arrive at success in
life.

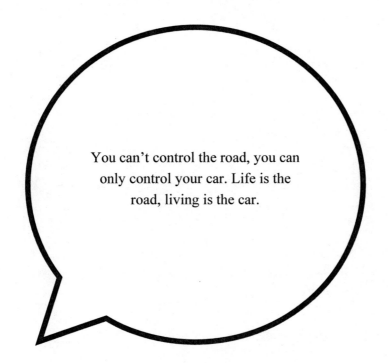

You can't control the road, you can only control your car. Life is the road, living is the car.

Life!

Love. Inspire. Flourish. Evolve.

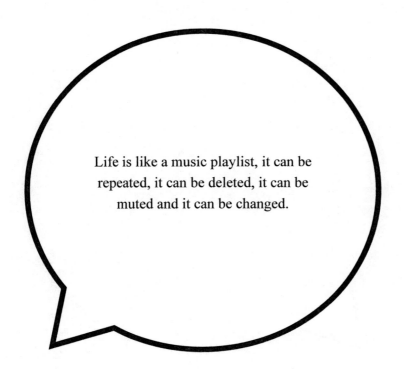

Life is like a music playlist, it can be repeated, it can be deleted, it can be muted and it can be changed.

Life's experience is the most intimate
form of understanding.

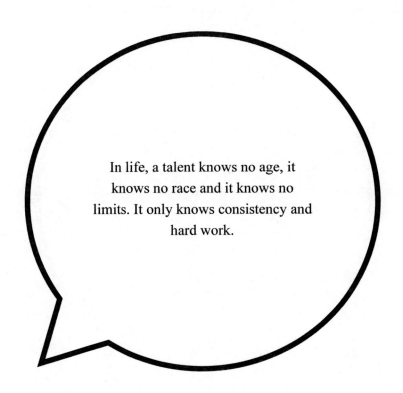

In life, a talent knows no age, it knows no race and it knows no limits. It only knows consistency and hard work.

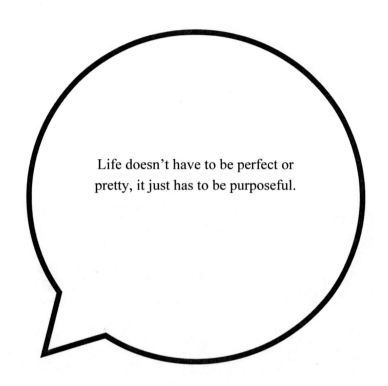

Life doesn't have to be perfect or pretty, it just has to be purposeful.

When life gives you a chance, big or small, break limits and make history.

In life, be anything but less.

In life, greatness is not born, greatness
is bred.

New Me!

Never ever worry.

To begin a new year, one has to end an old lifestyle.

Success starts with starting a new page a day, a new step a day, a new sacrifice a day, a new storm a day and a new you a day.

A new mind transforms you into a
new living.

Belief recycles your mind anew.

A candle is useful until it becomes windy; be ready to shine again, be sufficiently prepared and be motivated always.

Scared of a new idea? It is possible to have an idea and not have an idea about your idea, but it is a new start.

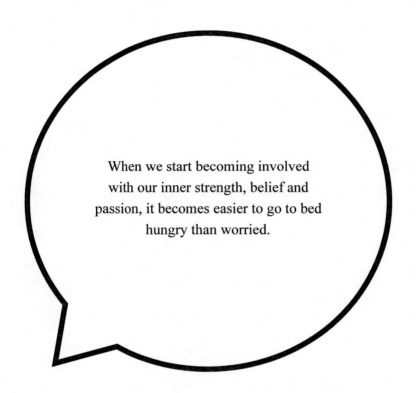

When we start becoming involved
with our inner strength, belief and
passion, it becomes easier to go to bed
hungry than worried.

Happiness!

Happiness is a journey without destination, just discoveries.

Happiness is created, not found.

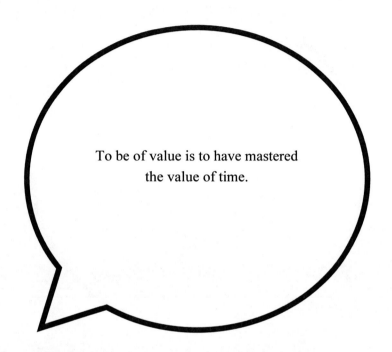

To be of value is to have mastered
the value of time.

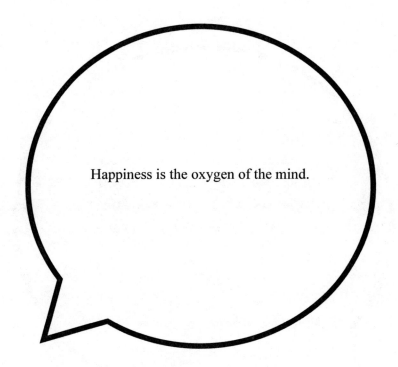

Happiness is the oxygen of the mind.

If you want to be happy, be yourself, trust yourself, build yourself, love yourself, value you and fight for you.

The first rule of having more is being happy with little.

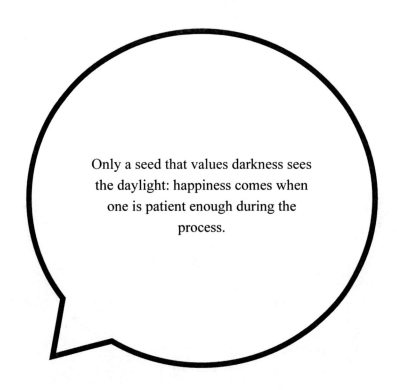

Only a seed that values darkness sees the daylight: happiness comes when one is patient enough during the process.

If you want to be happy, disconnect
yourself from unhappy minds.

Free!

Feeling right everyday everywhere.

Doing the things you love helps you
manage the things you must do.

Don't just be skilful, be useful.

Life is too short to be short-changing you, live adventurously.

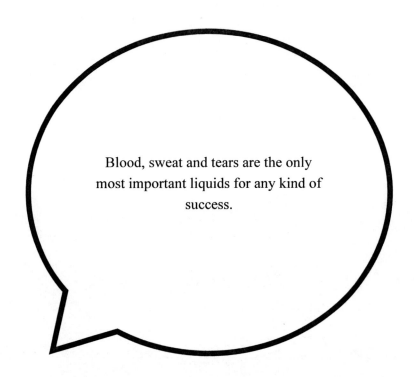

Blood, sweat and tears are the only most important liquids for any kind of success.

An extraordinary life starts with doing
the little ordinary things a little extra.

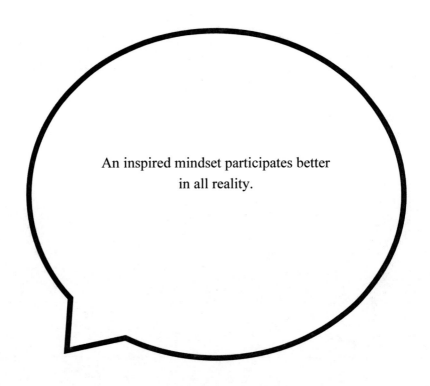

An inspired mindset participates better
in all reality.

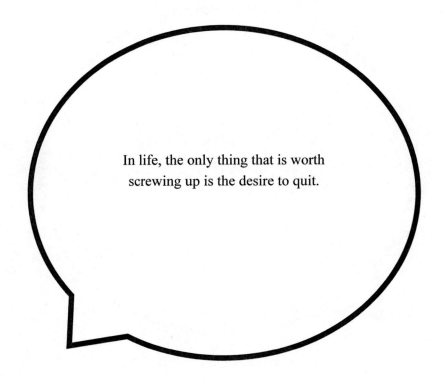

In life, the only thing that is worth
screwing up is the desire to quit.

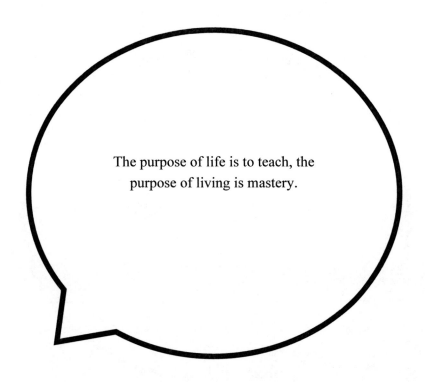

The purpose of life is to teach, the
purpose of living is mastery.

Home!

Home is my favourite feeling.

Home is the last stop of the day, make yours homely.

Home is an emotional adventure of memories, and a journey of love, unity, sadness, happiness, refuge, challenge, comfort, struggle, conquest, security.

Home is a final destination of belonging.

Home is hope, it is a wonderful
feeling of tomorrow.

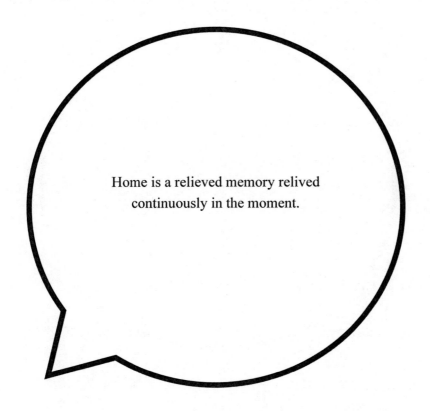

Home is a relieved memory relived
continuously in the moment.

The Voice of Life-Changing Moments!

The transition from ordinary to extraordinary requires thinking, learning, believing, having an inspired passion and working consistently hard.

Somewhere at this very moment, someone has the audacity and courage and is now very busy writing down their plans, visualising their goals and working very hard to execute them, and in a few years' time, they will become a better version of themselves and be somewhere, where you too would be if you would start writing yours down now.

- The next story we need to read is the one we write ourselves: you have a story in you. You just need to find your voice in words.
- Faith is like a knotweed, it pulls you through the cracks, no matter the strength of the darkness, no matter the strength of the obstacle.
- Destiny is the creation of habits.
- Have the courage of a seed and the patience of a farmer.
- Courage conquers challenges.
- Imagine, like medicine heals the world.
- Without a set goal, life's purpose becomes like a passing smoke rising up just to be gone.
- Experience is education and education is experience, whichever one is available right now should be taken advantage of tentatively.
- If you want to influence the world one day, work hard on you every day.
- Hard work is how inner strength is discovered.
- The most important moment in your life is now.
- It is dangerous not to have goals, not to dream.

- Find your Why. If you don't have a Why, the What or the Who won't get you there.
- Before you gain, you have to grit; before you grow, you have to get started.
- Put your originality out there. Someone is looking for you. They are waiting on you.
- Dreamers don't sleep too long. They don't wake too late.
- Creativity is all about four things: courage, craziness, consistency and hard work.
- Be desperate to win; sometimes, when you are desperate, you are driven.
- You need motivation to finish what you need to finish, not start it. To start, you just need a wish, a goal, a plan and start.
- Have a dream strong enough to get you out of bed and write.
- Be behind on your bills, not your best.
- Embrace your situation but never accept it.
- Sometimes, we have to dust certain people away in our life to see the true beauty of our surface once again.
- You have to give to get; sometimes it might be the little and the all you've got left.
- The difference between a thousand pound and a billion pound business profit is a notebook filled with thoughts and ideas.
- Understanding is a necessity; otherwise, knowledge will be a waste.
- When you start and quit, you acquire regret; but when you start and finish, you acquire result.
- Utilise disbelief. Disbelief can be a powerful motivator if applied positively. Sometimes, it is people's disbelief that pushes us to the limit and makes us go over our own limits.
- Time is the evidence of equal opportunity. Use yours wisely.
- If you stick around long enough and survive the challenges, the criticism, the lack of support, the small beginnings, the doubts— you will inevitably reap the rewards of your effort.
- The forward motion of time in practicality is a mindset, not a set of numbers.

- Accomplishment is all about attitude and action inspired by belief and driven by commitment.
- Be committed. Commitment is being exhausted by/from something you have been doing for a while but still waking up the next day working hard at it with passion.
- Comparison is the measure of appreciation.
- Sometimes, it is not passion or commitment that gets us out of bed to do the things that we must do, it is the consequences that would otherwise follow.
- Always invest in what you believe in; the greater the responsibility, the greater the opportunity.
- If a coin can land on one side, it can also land on the other side. If we can fail at something, we can also succeed at that same thing. It's all a matter of patience, efforts and attempts.
- Time is a mindset, not a set of numbers.
- The days you can't think or do positively, just listen positively.
- Where we are does not define where we get to, it is what we do where we are and who we become along the way that determines our destination.
- Small achievements drive big accomplishments.
- Be proud of getting out of bed today, it is the most important achievement of the day.
- It does not take much to start, but it takes everything (experience, knowledge, instinct support and positive emotions) to finish.
- Sometimes you have to break your bank account to break your limit.
- If you ever desperately need to be encouraged, listen to your own heartbeat.
- Love is not literature but biological.
- You can't get to the end if you quit halfway, and you can't quit halfway and get to the end.
- Be tired, be angry, be exhausted, be lonely, be confused, be mad, be overwhelmed or overworked, but never quit until you are accomplished.
- Don't worry about the whole week, just three days: yesterday, today and tomorrow.

- Success is not the final destination, knowledge and experience is.
- Stay in control: you can't handle success if you can't handle stress.
- Success is the arguments we had in our mind and won.
- Defeat is not an excuse to quit but a reason to come back better prepared.
- Defeat gives us the ability of foresight if we use the lessons learned or earned from it.
- Quitting is the point at which failure becomes permanent.
- Make positive memories out of mistakes, never regret going for something you once wanted, at least you dared yourself to have a go. You believed in you for once. Do it again.
- Don't be carried away by problems that you lose awareness of your own strength.
- There is something different about defeat; it makes you realise that there is more in you than you've always thought you had in you: it brings out the next big fighter out of you.
- Wake up every day and say, 'today is inevitable, it is my day to make'.
- Success is the consequence of courage.
- Defeat is just as effective and winning. The key is whatever comes first, learn from it and take it to the next level.
- When defeat occurs, you don't win by getting back up after a defeat. You win by working hard on improving yourself before the next try.
- If you want to win and win all the time, appreciate defeat.
- Only a serious mind wins.
- Quitting is only permissible if you can come up with 100 different reasons why you shouldn't try again.
- Success is a consequence of discipline in attitude and gratitude.
- Success requires you to stop talking and start taking actions, to stop wishing and start working harder.
- Success is like a Chinese bamboo tree, it does not show until the planting is done right and the timing is right to show.
- Leadership is success, it is the product of disciple.

- If you want to be a great leader, you have to be the best follower in the war room. If you want to be a great teacher, you have to be the best student in the classroom.
- The best gifts we can give our children are time, love, belief and a sound education.
- At the centre of leadership is replication. Lead to breed: don't just teach, transform; don't just instruct, inspire.
- Few years from now, your thoughts will become your trophy.
- You are more successful if you tried and failed than if you never tried at all.
- If you are not inspired, sooner or later you are going to quit trying.
- Motivation is the fuel of progress.
- Ambition is the best way to measure performance and improvement.
- The first achievement of a new year is surviving the last year.
- Never give up. Step up.
- If you can't find a way out, stop looking and start thinking.
- Always create time to think, not to worry but to think.
- Stay in control. Control is the courage to step up and step in, it is the mentality of entitlement, of ownership.
- Wake up every day, touch gloves with life and control your battles.
- Fear has no significance when courage speaks.
- Feedback is among the greatest gifts you can receive, use it well and use all of it.
- Without understanding, failure becomes repetitive and replicable.
- A new chapter starts with courage and faith.
- Prepare before you waken up: preparation predicts performance.
- Stop giving excuses: excuse is what we provide when we are not seriously ready to progress; plan is what we provide when we are ready to help ourselves.
- Never settle: when you settle too soon, life comes in too early and stays longer than expected, sometimes even permanently.
- Talent mixed with education puts you on a different podium.
- If you don't have the right people to help you, rely on the right books.

- At the end of the day, everyone ends up back in their mind. Make sure yours is a better home.
- If they tell you no, make them wish they hadn't. Work harder, do better, do it yourself.
- If you can't admire great work, you simply can't achieve great work.
- If you really want to be happy, set goals: happiness is found in the company of achievement.
- Let your I define your Me.
- At some point in life, we learn what matters the most: peace, family, love and thyself.
- Negativity is negativity. Cut loose. No one has the right to put all your efforts down just because they are your blood. No one, no exception.
- If you haven't been through hell or hardship, you will never know how to make life count.
- Have your you time, reflect on your life: sometimes the best time to pay attention and listen is when no one is speaking.
- Freedom is not when we are let loose. Freedom is when we let ourselves loose.
- Start now, later is too uncertain, too unpredictable.
- Success comes from different backgrounds, never let where you are stop you from where you can be: you can influence the world from the side-lines.
- Something powerful begins to happen when you have a message to share. You start drifting from courage to recklessness until your goal is achieved.
- Stay educated: education is essential for human struggle, survival and success.
- Awareness through knowledge is the best form of help or self-help.
- Happiness is the product of knowledge. If you are not happy, you've got a lot to learn.
- Friendship is the most important part of happiness.
- Friendship is an adventurous ship in the ocean of life.
- Silence is the most powerful voice of strength.

- Hard work is a distraction from discouraging voices.
- Doubt is the voice of limitation.
- Your perception has everything to do with your progression: be inspired, be motivated, be knowledgeable.
- Nothing is more responsible for happiness than self-discovery and self-worth.
- Friendship makes life a two-way journey.
- The best way to feel good is to feel free.
- Team work is how ordinary people achieve extraordinary performance.
- Every day, work hard, ignore the pain and be inspired by the gain.
- The best part about day one is that it can be any day, anytime, like right now.
- When you finally meet the best version of you, you will never feel alone or lonely.
- Motivation is like factory settings, it brings you back to your best natural state.
- A positive change in your mentality changes your reality a little better day by day.
- The strength you feel in you is what you see when you look at your reflection.
- There is positivity in everything, negativity is no exception.
- The best view of the world is through your imagination.
- Sometimes life gives you a process before a purpose: so whatever you do, make sure you are learning, never lose the lesson.
- Excuse is what we provide when we are not seriously ready to progress; plan is what we provide when we are ready to help ourselves.
- Work hard: preparation predicts performance.
- Every day is a wakeup call to live more, love more, learn more and level up.
- You are not a problem but a working project, a process in progress.

- Don't be scared to show off, someone out there needs to be inspired by exceptionality today.
- Don't pray to have, pray to become.
- The only equal opportunity for mankind is time. Don't give yours away foolishly.
- Discovery is an act of selflessness.
- A new year does not exist at the absence of a new mindset.
- If your grass loses colour and you move to a new one without changing your mindset, the new grass will meet the same fate as the old grass.
- Procrastination is a product of creativity: the mouse never stops in its wheel because it never stops to think.

Lastly, to the World at Large

In times of global adversities, stay united, stay strong and stay safe, that is the first cure, the first solution.

Create a positive change by sharing love and loving one another in times of peace, not just in times of adversity. In essence, the sad truth is that on a global scale, only misery has had the power to bring humans consciously closer and connected so far. And it is during global adversity that humans tend to appreciate the little things we've always taken for granted, things like unity, peace, valuable information, education, experience, justice, love, time out and self-care. Live life fully with love in your mind, love in your heart and love in your action.

Thank You